Reading and Interpreting the Bible in African Indigenous Churches

By

Prof. David Tuesday Adamo PhD

Wipf and Stock Publishers
150 West Broadway • Eugene OR 97401
2001

Reading and Interpreting the Bible in African Indigenous Churches

By Adamo, David Tuesday
Copyright©2001 by Adamo, David Tuesday
ISBN: 1-57910-700-1

Printed by *Wipf and Stock Publishers*
150 West Broadway • Eugene OR 97401

Table of Contents

DEDICATION

This book is dedicated to
Rev Dr. Lee W and Dessie Pearl Turner of
Lee Turner Ministries and New Mount Zion Missionary Baptist
Church
Waxachie, Texas

ACKNOWLEDGMENTS

I would like to appreciate my wife Grace Ebunlola Adamo who did the editing of this book. I am also grateful to Lee Turner Ministries and the entire New Mount Zion Missionary Church, Waxahachie, Texas for their kind assistance during my stay in the United States.

I owe my friend, Pauline Nolly Logan my praise for not only reading this manuscript, but also for allowing God to use her to save my life. She will always be remembered Texas for their kind assistance for my stay in the United States.

I am grateful to Mr. Yemi Sanni, Mr. & Mrs Segun Okesanya, and Dr. Daniel Metzger whom God has used to safe my life in America.

My university, Delta State University, Abraka, Nigeria, deserves my appreciation for giving me an extended sabbatical leave that enables me to write this book.

Above all, to God be the Praise and glory.

David Tuesday Adamo PhD
Delta State University
Abraka, Nigeria.

CHAPTER I

INTRODUCTION

It is an indisputable fact that Africa is the cradle of biblical interpretation. As early as the first century biblical interpretation flourished in Africa in the University of Alexandria in Africa.[1] The unfortunate fact is that most Eurocentric biblical scholars presented North Africa as if it is part of Europe. Worse still, they presented many of the early biblical scholars in the University of Alexandria as Western scholars rather than African scholars. Yet, we know that most of these early biblical scholars in Alexandria were Africans. Most of them were born, worked, and lived in Africa. Some of these early biblical interpreters were presented as Jews and as if African people could not be Jewish. Although some of them were Jewish, that does not mean that they were not Africans. The Falashas from Ethiopia, the Lemba in South Africa who have been recently genetically (DNA) confirmed to be authentically orthodox Jews attest to the fact that Africans could be Jews.[2] Basilides, Pantaenus, Clement of Alexandria, Origen, Tertullian, Cyprian of Carthage, Carpocrates, Valentinus, Didymus the Blind, Arius, Athanasius, Cyril of Alexandria, and Augustine of Hippo are distinguished African biblical scholars who have made substantial contributions to early biblical interpretation. The influence of their interpretation on the world of biblical scholarship during their time cannot be overestimated.[3] These African scholars established their distinctive African biblical interpretation. Their methods of interpretation, though mostly allegorical, literal, and criticized as heretic, became the foundation of the Western modern biblical interpretation today.

Some early Western missionaries and anthropologists "smothered what is positive in African indigenous religious system." Everything African was considered as of no significance and are and their achievements were attributed to someone else. Their social systems were considered not worth maintaining. African life was also described as irrational.[4] This has been the unfortunate attitude of the Western-oriented churches in Africa whose sympathy lye with the so-called Western modern thought.

The biblical interpretation and the structure of the Western oriented churches in Africa are becoming progressively a suspect.[5] The imposition of Western values and institutions on indigenous African systems is a major cause of the retrogression of the so-called mainline churches. At the coming of the missionaries, the organization of the church as an institution appeared to be more important to the missionaries than the traditional inborn sense of fellowship, care, and sharing that are basic in traditional African religion. These are values that African Indigenous churches addressed when they were established.

Although the majority of African biblical scholars today are beneficiaries of the Western biblical interpretation as a result of access to the Western education, they are not passive receivers of western biblical interpretation. African biblical scholars have recognized that the value of any biblical studies depends on its relevance to the life of members of the communities where it is applied. We have recognized that many of the Western biblical interpretations and theologies nourished in the Western intellectualist context can have no roots in the life of the African communities. We also have recognized that any biblical interpretation is relevant only if it helps Africans to formulate their own problems more clearly. If not, it becomes very unprofitable to produce biblical studies or theologies for its own sake. Biblical studies must be relevant to the cultural and religious situation of the community that produced it. We also recognize that the imposition of Western values and institutions on indigenous

African systems is a major cause of the retrogression of the mainline churches in Africa. The recognition of these facts has led us "to create an encounter between biblical text and African context" in order to focus mainly (not in exclusion of other factors) on the community that received the text rather than on the one that produced it.[6]

In this book, I want to attempt to present how the African indigenous churches have been able to resolve the identity crisis engendered by the Western missionary biblical and theological position, through bringing the African value system of traditional religion into their interpretation of the Bible and of Christianity. To put it in another way, this book is an honest discussion on how the African indigenous churches have been able to use the fundamental principle of traditional African religion, after it has been analyzed and integrated, into Christianity in Africa.

The mainline churches have neglected human needs at the very grassroots level, as a result of copying the Western biblical interpretation and theology. This book wants to attempt to examine how the African indigenous churches, which have often been alienated from the rank and file, for upholding African traditional human values, have reacted by caring and sharing fellowship with members who have accepted the reconstruction to their churches.

This book is part of the Africentric approaches to biblical studies. It attempts to enhance our sense of worth as persons, as people among groups who are trying to make sense of our Christian and cultural values. I must say that this approach (Africentrism) does not deny or degrade other people's approaches in biblical studies. To put it in another way, it does not negate Eurocentrism, except where Eurocentrism to biblical studies attempt to claim universalism at the exclusion of Africentrism.[7] This book is important because it addresses the matter pertaining to culture. Every human being belongs to a culture in either his or her own culture, or other person's culture. But it is essential to participate in a culture or multiculture.

I am interested in contributing to the present trend in

biblical studies in Africa. As a scholar I am interested in studying not how scholars interpret the Bible alone, but how the ordinary people read and interpret it. This method will be of great value anywhere in the world because the majority of the people who study the Bible are ordinary readers. African scholars are not satisfied with scholars approach alone, but also with the ordinary people, that is, those who are not trained as professional biblical scholars.

In order to achieve the above objectives, this book attempts to answer the following questions. Why are African indigenous people satisfied with meeting in "shacks, shelters made from motorcar boxes in open spaces, school class rooms, and along the beaches.?"[8] In African Christianity "an action is judged right or wrong depending on the extent to which it promoted well-being, mutual understanding and social harmony.[9] How were African Indigenous Churches able to revive the African moral value system, which has humankind at heart? How were they able to use the interpretation of the Bible and Christianity to meet the need of those who feel disjointed, and out of gear; and who lack progress because of the Western church institution and theology. As Eurocentric interpreters express their culture by using literary allusions, illustrations, and figures that emerge from their cultural experiences, should African Christians be allowed to use their African cultural experiences in their interpretation of the Bible? Molefi Asante is right when he says, "If your God cannot speak to you in your language, then he is not your God."[10] Should Africans be appreciated as they serve God and interpret the Bible and Christianity in their own language, in the language of their ancestors, and in the language with which God spoke to them?

My readers should understand that this book is not a systematic discussion of my credo, but an honest account of many years of research among people in Nigeria who have reacted courageously and positively and established African Indigenous churches and made positive use of their God-given culture for the benefit of their people and the world. The main churches visited are: Cherubim and Seraphim Churches, Celestial Church of Christ,

Church of the Lord Aladura, and Christ Apostolic Church. According to my observation, these are the most active and aggressive African Indigenous Churches in Nigeria. I, therefore, use them as representative of the rest of the churches in Africa. The major characteristics of these churches, as will be discussed in this book, run through most of the rest of the African Indigenous churches in Africa. Admittedly, there may be exceptions but they are usually few. Whatever academic sin of omission and/or generalization committed, I would like to bear the full responsibility.

Chapter one is the basic introduction to this book. Chapter two discusses the main outline of African worldview as a useful background to the understanding of the why, nature, practices, and mode of interpretation of the Bible in African Indigenous churches. Chapter three gives a brief survey of African Indigenous churches. (Christ Apostolic Church (CAC), Cherubim and Seraphim, Church of the Lord, Aladura, and Celestial Church of Christ CCC).

Chapter four deals with how African indigenous churches read and interpret the Bible therapeutically. It discusses how the Bible has been used to solve health problems in a society where everybody does not have access to modern orthodox medicine.

Chapter five is also a discussion of how African worldview and traditional culture have been used in conjunction with the Bible for the purpose of protection against all kinds of evil that plague humankind.

Chapter six is a demonstration of how African indigenous Churches read and interpret the Bible as a means of achieving success in all life endeavors.

Chapter seven is the evaluation of my basic understanding of the African indigenous biblical hermeneutics. The main essence (names, power of words, faith, prayer, and God's power) of this hermeneutics is emphasized.

I hope this book would stimulate serious reflection on the approach of African indigenous churches to biblical studies. As in my other previous books,[11] my readers should relax whatever is their previous opinion about Africa and their tradition when they read this book in order to appreciate it. Whether Eurocentric biblical scholars appreciate or accept what African biblical scholars have to say or not, we must continue to affirm what needs to be said, be who we are, and write what we must write in order to keep and extend our sanity.[12]

Endnotes

[1] J.S Ukpong, "Development in Biblical Interpretation in Africa: A Historical and Hermeneutical Directions," *The Bible in Africa* (New York: E J Brill, 2000), 11

[2] See David Adamo, *Africa and Africans in the New Testament*, to be published by Judson Press. See also Magdel Le Roux, " 'Lost Tribes of Israel' in Africa? Some observations on Judaising Movements in Africa, with Specific Reference to the Lemba in South Africa," *Religion Theology*, Volume 6-2 (1999), 102-139

[3] Bruce Metzger, *Canon of the New Testament:Its Origin, Development, and Significance* (Oxford: Claredon Press, 1997), 129-142; 156-163, Maureen A. Tilley, *The Bible in Christian North Africa, The Donatist World* (Minneapolis: Fortress Press, 1996), Donald K. McKim, ed. *Historical Handbook of Major Biblical Interpreters* (Downers Grove, Illinois: 1998).

[4] G.C Oosthuizen, "The Task of African Traditional Religion in the Church's Dilemma in South Africa," in *African Spirituality: Forms, Meaning, and Expressions*, edited by Jacob Olupona (New York: Crossroad Publishing Company, 2000), 277-283

[5] Ibid.,

[6] Ukpong, See also Holter, LeMarguand and others in *The Bible in Africa (New York: E. Brill, 2000),*

[7] The word "Afrocentrism" was coined by Molefi Asante. See his book *The Afrocentric Idea* (Philadelphia: Temple University Press, 1987). See also J.

Endnotes

Deotis Roberts who prefers "Africentrism" to "Afrocentrism," *Africentric*

Christianity, (Valley Forge: Judson Press, 2000)

[8] G.C Oosthuizen, "The Task of African Traditional Religion in the Church's Dilema in South Africa," in *African Spirituality: Forms, Meaning and Expressions*, edited by Jacob Olupona (New York: Cross Road Publishing Company, 2000), 277-283

[9] Ibid. 281

[10] *Afrocentricity*, rev. ed. (Trenton,NJ: Africa World Press, 1988), 2

[11] David Adamo, *African American Heritage?* (Eugene, OR: WIPF& Stock Publishers. 2001); *Africa and Africans in the Old Testament*, Bethesda, MD:University Press of America, 1998) reprinted by WIPF and Stock and Publishers, Eugene, Oregon, 2001.

; David Adamo, *Africa and Africans in the New Testament* (Valley Forge: Judson Press, to be published, 2002), David Adamo, *Exploration in African Biblical Studies* (Eugene, Oregon: WIPF &Stock Publishers to be published 2001).

[12] J. Deotis Roberts, *Africentric Christianity*, 11

CHAPTER II

AFRICAN WORLDVIEW

My discussion of the use of Bible therapeutically, protectively, and as success in life in African Indigenous Churches cannot be properly understood without a discussion of African worldview in general and as it concerns healing, protection and success. African worldview is the basic context of the interpretation of the Bible therapeutically, and the means of protection and success in life by African Indigenous Churches. Indigenous churches that I visited and discussed, have their origin among the Yoruba people of Nigeria, I will dwell more on the Yoruba worldview.

The Structure of the Universe

The Yoruba people of Nigeria are one of the largest nations on the continent of Africa. They live in the southwestern part of Nigeria, Republic of Benin and Togo. Their indigenous religious system is born out of experience with God that has been handed down from generation to generation. There are myths, folklores, songs, dances, rites, rituals, proverbs, adages and liturgies. The Yoruba people strongly believe in predestination. Everyone chooses his or her destiny before his birth. Although some believe that this destiny cannot be changed, the majority believes that through prayer, supernatural, and special ritual actions, each person's destiny can be altered or redefined.[1]

The Yoruba people have a complex religious system and a complex concept of the universe. These can be illustrated in the form of "pyramidal structure as shown below.

GOD (*Olodumare*)

DIVINITIES (*Awon Orisa*)

SPIRITS (*Awon Emi*)

ANCESTORS (The Living Dead)

KINGS, PRIESTS, CHIEFS, QUEENS, RULERS, Devotee

The occupant of the highest place is God who is the Supreme Being called *Olorun* or *Olodumare*. The Divinities are called *Orisas* and occupy the second level in Yoruba religious system. The third position in the order of things belongs to the spirits called *Emi*. The ancestors who are referred to as the "Living-Dead" occupy the fourth position. They are not considered supernatural beings like he occupants of the first, second, and third positions. Special human beings who are rulers, kings, priests, queens, and chiefs are in the fifth position. They are living beings. The devotees occupy the sixth place.

In my discussion of African worldview, attention would be given to African medicine. The meaning, classification, and the use of it will be discussed. I consider this to be very important because the reading and interpretation of the Bible in African Indigenous churches have some affinities with African medicine.

God

Like the Biblical Hebrew, the existence of God in Africa is assumed. In fact, the question of the existence of God is not disputed. The idea that He is the creator of the heavens and earth and of human being is not disputed in African Indigenous religion.

This idea of Him as the creator and the final authority is expressed in the names given to Him in Africa.   For example, the Yoruba people of Nigeria call Him *Olodumare* which means He is Almighty and supreme; *Olorun*, the owner of heaven; *Eleda*, the creator and maker; *Alaaye*, the living One; *Elemi*, the owner of spirit or breath. Among the Yoruba people of Nigeria, it is believed that these names of God are potent. It is believed that these names could perform some miracles and bring blessing. Among the Ibos of Nigeria, He is called *Chineke*, creator; *Onyeokike*, the person who creates; *Chukwu*, Great Spirit; *Osebuluwa*, Lord who upholds the world. Among the Sierra Leonians He is called *Leve-* supreme creator, the one who is high up; *Ngewo-* God, Great Spirit. Among the Ghanians He is called *Onyame-*The Supreme Being, the creator of all things; *Mawu-*God *Mawuga-* the Great God; *Se-* The Supreme God. There are so many names of God in African indigenous tradition that we cannot name all of them here.[2]

His attributes are also many. He is the creator of the heavens and the earth. He is also in control of all things. He knows and sees all things. He is all-powerful. Even though He is far away He is also present everywhere. He is the first and the last cause. He is a spirit and can appear to human being at any time and in any place. He is king. He is judge and immortal. He is holy. Among the Yoruba people of Nigeria these attributes are expressed in songs, dances, adages, ritual actions, and others. He can use any means to heal, to protect and to deliver, to punish and to bless. He is the final protector. He can use water, sand, prayers, potent words, wood, plant, leaves, angels, man or woman to protect, to heal and to bring success. He is the king and master. His name is sacred. The names He gives to things are sacred. It is quite remarkable that there is no image of God. Unlike the Eurocentric concept of God, He is not a philosophical entity.

Divinities

God has divinities.   These divinities are His instrument and messengers. These divinities have their local names in local villages according to the functions assigned to them. These divinities are real in the minds of the believers. They are personification of God. While some divinities have the functions of healing, others have that of protecting and granting success in all human endeavors. Among the Yoruba people of Nigeria, the divinities are the *Orisas*. The names include *Orisa nla, Ogun, Oshun, Ela, Sango, Esu, Sonpona, Orunmila*. These divinities have special relationship with *Olodumare*. All these have special functions assigned to them by *Olodumare*.[3]

Spirits

God, who is a spirit, also has some category of spirits of which He is the chief. These spirits are apparitional entities. They are immaterial or incorporeal beings. Everything in the world has a spirit. These spirits are also divided into different categories according to their functions. There are spirits of witches, born-to-die spirits (*abiku*), guardian spirits for healing, protection and success. Although they do not seem to make sense to the western mind, yet they exist. In the African mind it does not make sense to ask whether they exist or not. There are spirits of water called *Yemoja* among the Yorubas of Nigeria; *Ota Miri* among the Ibos of Nigeria, *Tano* of the Akan of Ghana. Human beings also have spirits. All the divinities have their own spirits.

Ancestors

There is a strong belief in ancestors who are referred to as the living-dead. Those who are dead are believed to have gone to a different world of existence. This is the world of spiritual existence. The ancestors who once lived among human being have now gone to the spiritual existence and are watching over their human family. All the dead people are not ancestors. They have to fulfill certain conditions, which include old age, good, and honorable character during their time on earth. They must die certain type of death. Wicked people cannot become ancestors.

Every family has ancestors who communicate, guard, and punish whenever necessary. The ancestors also have the function of protecting the family from dangers.

There are priests assigned to these divinities, spirits, and ancestors. By the permission of God these priests have special relationship with the divinities, ancestors and spirits. These priests were taught medicine for healing, protection, and success. They are also given the responsibilities of healing the people,, protedting them and helping them to achieve success using herbal and social and psychological means. However, the indigenous Africans ultimate protection rest upon God. In this case, the priests have special relationship to God, the divinities, spirits, and the ancestors.

Medicine

The early study of African indigenous medicine has been subjected to various interpretations by various groups of people-colonialists, traders, anthropologists, and missionaries. Due to lack of adequate understanding of the nature of African medicine and culture, African indigenous medicine has been branded mere fetishism, magic superstition, animism, witchcraft, and sorcery. The medicine men and women are therefore also branded witch doctors, magicians, and other weird names that cannot be adequately substantiated. Some examples of these early men include Une Maclean. He classified "magical" medicine as "irrationality, malpractice, and a mixture of superstition, deliberate deception and ignorance."[4] E.B Tylor was also quick to describe it "a monstrous farrago" that does not contain any iota of truth or value.[5] Scholars like Gelfand called the African medicine man and woman, witch doctors.[6]

The missionaries whom Africans expected would study African culture and understand African indigenous religion better does not seem to do better. Even as late as the 20th century, they still forbade their converts from using indigenous medicine with a serious threat of excommunication from the church and the consequence of hell fire. M. M Iwu gives an accurate description of the majority of the foreigner's picture of African indigenous medicine and medicine men and women when he says:

The popular image of the African medicine man is that of fabled witch doctor, with his exotic paraphernalia of feathers, cowries and animal sting muttering meaningless incantations and dispensing worthless portions to equally ignorant clients. Even the herbs they dispensed are considered harmful and when they are found efficacious, the detractors of traditional medicine are quick to dismiss them as chance discovery. The incantations and the rhythm of drums are said to be weird sounds and part of the mubo-jubo designs to hoodwink the superstitions savages who are under their spell.[7]

However, the 20th century Africans began to witness serious efforts to study African indigenous medicinal plants. This is partly because many diseases are becoming resistant to synthetic medicine and the realization that the year 2000 target which WHO set for "Health for ALL" is impossible with the use of synthetic medicine, all over the world, particularly, in Africa. Many serious attempts have also been made to study Yoruba, Igbo and Urhobo medicinal plants.[8] Scholars such as Iwu, Ezeabalisili, Sofola, Ayoade, Dopamu, Maclean, and Ubrurhe should be commended for these efforts.[9]

Definition of Indigenous Medicine

No matter how despicable the knowledge of orthodox and modern scientific medicine is in Africa, the fact is that the world is indebted to Africa for at least the rudiments of this art of medicine.[10] Africa once led the world in civilization and the knowledge of medicine through Egypt.[11] In the light of this, the word "indigenous medicine " is preferred because it
portrays better the idea that African indigenous medicine means the medicine that actually originated from Africa and passed from generations to generations.
According to *Concise Oxford Dictionary*, medicine is "an art of restoring and preserving health, especially by means of remedial

subsistence of regulation of diet as opposed to surgery and obstetric." It goes further to define medicine from the perspective of the less privileged people as "spell," "charms," and "fetish." Without question this definition is inadequate from the African perspective. Medicine in African perspective is not only therapeutic. Even from the less privileged perspective, medicine is not only "spells," "charms," and "fetish." According to *Webster's New World Dictionary of the American Language*,[12] medicine is "a science and art of diagnosing, treating, curing, and preventing disease, relieving pain, improving and preserving health." It goes further to define medicine as "any drug or other substance used in treating disease, healing or relieving pain." The dictionary also defines medicine from the less privileged perspective as "any object, spell, rite and so on supposed to have natural supernatural powers as a remedy, preventive and so on." Although, there is an improvement in the above definition by defining medicine to include the word, "diagnosing," "rite," it still falls short of what I think should be the correct meaning of indigenous medicine in African perspective. It still sees medicine as essentially therapeutic and preventive.

Many definitions of medicine by African scholars are equally defective. Dopamu defines medicine in African context as "the art of using available resources of nature to prevent, treat or cure disease.[13] Mume, Metuh, and Sofowora's definitions are very instructive. According to Mume, indigenous medicine (he uses traditional) "is the transmission by word of mouth and by example the knowledge and practice based on customary methods of natural healing or treatment of disease."[14] Sofowora defines medicine as the " total combination of knowledge and practice whether explicable or not, used in diagnosing, preventing or eliminating a physical, mental or social disease and which may rely exclusively on past experience and observation handed down from generation to generation verbally or in writing."[15] Professor Ikenga Metuh's is most instructive. According to him, indigenous medicine is "anything that can be used to heal, to kill, secure power, health, fertility, personality or moral reforms."[16] This includes anything that has the so-called magic effect. In his definition he rightly observed that African indigenous medicine includes not only herbal mixture, but also the so -called "magical" objects, incantation, and rites capable of affecting human condition either for good or for worse. Professor A.B.T Byaruhanga-Akiki's definition of indigenous medicine is also instructive. It is "the act of curing man's disharmony with himself, another person, nature and environment."[17] In order to restore this disharmony there is the need for the use of humankind, animal and plant.

Prof. Dopamu's definition of indigenous medicine, though an improvement on the *Concise Oxford Dictionary*, and Websters Dictionary is inadequate. His definition is also basically therapeutic. It is one for preventing, treating and healing. Mume's definition reflects actual meaning of traditional and not indigenous as defined above. He emphasizes transmission by word of mouth and practice of natural method of healing. It is a very vague definition and therapeutic only. So also is Sofowora's definition. Prof. A.B.T Byaruhanga-Akiki's definition seems to fall into the same category as Dopamu's and others who see the function of medicine as essentially therapeutic. Professor Metuh's is the most instructive of all (except he uses traditional) as he defines indigenous medicine in a way that it does not only therapeutic, but involves the act of killing, securing power and moral reforms. In African context, medicine can certainly be used to kill, to cause diseases, to bring good luck or to be successful or find favor or love apart from its therapeutic function. I prefer the use of indigenous medicine when referring to African indigenous medicine. African indigenous medicine is the use of anything, material or immaterial, explicable or inexplicable, which originated and transmitted from generation to generation in order to treat, to heal, to kill, to punish, obtain success or good luck and general well being of people. This is how the word African indigenous medicine will be used here in this paper. There is the tendency for the West to see the so-called African magic as different from medicine. However, the use of magic is problematic.[18]

The Classification of Indigenous Medicine.

Since there are no clear-cut differences in the classification of the indigenous medicine, what I would like to do is to make an attempt to differentiate and group together some of these indigenous medicine for the purpose of identification. Professor Akiki identified three major classifications of African indigenous medicine- herbal medicine, ritual medicine, and mystical medicine.[19]

The first classification of African indigenous medicine is the herbal medicine. According to him this group of medicine is made from leaves, back of trees, plants, juices, and other parts of plants. They are mainly used for what Byaruhanga-Akiki calls biological diseases such as arthritis, asthma, diarrhea, eye diseases, pneumonia, cholera, malaria and other general diseases that cannot be named here.

The second type is the ritual medicine. This ritual medicine involves sacrifices, eating of some specific kind of food and giving various prescribed gifts. They are performed to heal social, psychological and psychosomatic diseases. In this case cows, sheep, goats, soil, chickens, snakes, cowhides, bones, and rocks may be used. Taboo is an essential part of human existence and therefore they must be obeyed. It is part of the ways by which order is maintained in the African society. Any breach of such taboos can result in social disorders, psychological and psychosomatic disease. Doctors in the orthodox western hospitals have not successfully treated such diseases. There are several cases in which after many examinations of the patients, they are told that "*ki ise aisan hospital ko*" (it is not a hospital disease).

The third type of medicine is mystical medicine (not magical medicine). This is what some Western and African scholars call "magic medicine." I will try to avoid this term because Western missionaries and anthropologists use it derogatorily. I will use instead the word "mystery medicine." This is because the earlier anthropologists, missionaries, and Europeans in general used the word to mean clever trickery, especially in conjuring tricks. It means a jumble of deceitful acts as it is known by the work of the western magicians who have perfected their tricks. Some early visitors to Africa who arrived in Africa witnessed some medicine men who performed their healing. These missionaries could not understand them because of the secrecy of their practice in an unhealthy environment. When they could not understand them they called them magicians. When they also encountered other false medicine men who were generally not effective, they concluded that African indigenous medicines are magic and those who practice them are witch doctors.

However, African indigenous medicine is not magic and should not be called magic. They may be involved in some secrecy or mystery, they are not meant for deceit. African medicine involves using herbs, roots, leaves, animal parts and general natural materials, to heal, to bring good luck (*awure*) sharp memory (*isoye*) to punish enemies, for good sales and for general protection, to secure love, to win lawsuit, to escape ghastly accident and escape death from war zone.[20] The white men labeled African indigenous medicine magic, because they regarded them as jumble of lies and deceit. The African medicine persons (*oologun* or *onisegun* or *elegbogi*) are mere trickers according to them. The mystical medicine includes curses, incantations and some rituals. Such medicine for retentive memory, good sales, love, escape from dangerous battle or ghastly accident and others are many. There are testimonies that despite the mystery that surrounds the medicine, they are efficacious.

I remember a story of a frustrated woman who cursed her husband and wanted to reverse the curse.[21] This woman who is from a rich family married a poor man. Her father built a house for them and bought many vehicles for the husband to use for transport business. They became very successful and bought additional vehicles and houses. The husband married five more wives and neglected the first one whose father bought a vehicle and a house for them. He forgot entirely that the father in-law was the source of their wealth despite the plea of his first wife. Eventually, he sent the first wife and her children out the matrimonial house.

She had no choice but to retaliate by cursing her husband. When it was exactly twelve midnight, she went naked at a certain crossroad, and with tears cursed her husband to return to poverty. The result was that few weeks later, all the man's vehicles had accidents beyond repairs. His houses got burnt. (unfortunately, many in the Third World do not care for insurance). But she could not bear the situation when she saw her husband's wretchedness. She wept and prayed for the reversion of the curse but it was impossible. This is a clear-cut example of a category of African indigenous medicine.

In this category, the use of potent words is most important because of the basic belief of Africans, especially the Yoruba people of Nigeria. Indigenous Africans believe that when we were born we were given some potent words. These words give us the power to balance both our spiritual and physical bodies and to awaken in us the highest potential in our soul. These potent words can be used for energy, prosperity, healing and protection. These words given to each person have unlimited possibilities within our incarnation for every one of us who are willing to make use of the words and who put forth some unique effort to remember the word for use. This effort includes attaching some spiritual significance to the words that we can remember for our use. African Indigenous people believe that "OUR VOICE IS our most creative instrument. With our words we can make others feel as if they are standing within God's shadow, or we can make them shrink as if they were some hideous being from Hell." They consider words as "mystical and magikal." All the ancient African mystery schools "taught their students about the power of the words." They taught that when a thought is expressed in words, it forms the matrix of what will manifest within our physical lives. This is the reason they all stressed resilience in speech at all times.[22]

Words are used not only to communicate with the human, but also with the divine beings. That is why in ancient and modern

art of communication, the essential power of sound and words is a common element. "Many of the ancient languages had a very sonorous effect when spoken, and had sounds of tremendous transmutative potential." The words and sign of these languages in many cases were designed for communication with the consciousness of the Angelic Kingdoms, and to
keep the soul in communication with the Divine while in the physical body."[23] This is not to say that our modern languages do not have the power. The art of empowering words may temporarily be put aside, obscured, hidden from the view, but it still exists. It can still be opened to people who are ready to learn the method and have the willingness to open the communication with the divine.

The process of empowering words in African indigenous religion is simple. It is through a combination of high standard of discipline through fasting, repetition of words, attaching definite meanings to sounds of the words and their combinations and performance of other rituals prescribed. When these words are "toned" and put in such a prescribed manner, the energy would be projected into the individual life circumstances and be grounded into the physical.

However, For the purpose of this book, I will prefer the classification of African Indigenous medicine as, first, Protective Medicine, second, Therapeutic medicine, and third, Success medicine. This classification will be fully explained in my discussion below.

The efficacy of the indigenous medicine was never doubted, not because orthodox medicine was not known to them but mainly for the fact that the indigenous medicine was efficacious. Despite the existence of orthodox medicine the indigenous one is still in use among the African people.

Endnotes

[1] The Yoruba people believe that when everyone was born, two types of destinies in covered dishes were placed before the individual to choose. Whichever one chooses would be the path that such individual would follow.

[2] Kofi Asare Opoku, *West African Traditional Religion* (Accra, Ghana: Fep International Private Ltd., 1978), 14-18

[3] E. Bolaji Idowu, *Olodumare, God in Yoruba Belief* (New York: Longmans, 1994)

[4] Una Maclean, *Magical Medicine: A Nigerian Case Study*, (London: Reading and Fakenham, 1971), 13.

[5] Quoted by R.R. Marret, "Magic," in *Encyclopedia of Religion and Ethics* , vol 8 ,James Hastings, ed (Edinburgh: T &T Clark, 1971),235.

[6] M.Gelfand, Medicine and Custom in Africa (Edinburgh: E. Livingstone, 1964), 137.

[7] M.M Iwu "Symbolism and Selectivity in Traditional African Medicines," A Lecture Delivered by the Winner of the Vice Chancellor's Research Leadership Prize for 1987 University of Nigerian, Nsukka, Nigeria, Jan. 12, 1988.

[8] M.M Iwu did some important researches in the field of Igbo traditional medicine, such as "Traditional Igbo Medicine ," A Report of a Project sponsored by the Institute of African Studies, University of Nigeria,(UNN),

Nsukka, Nigeria,1981, and "Symbolism and Selectivity, in Traditional African Medicine," delivered at UNN, 1989. See also P.A Dopamu, who published many articles such as " Health and Healing Within the Traditional African Religious Context," *Orita, vol 17(1985)*, "The Place of Onisegun in the Yoruba Health care System,"in *The Place of Religion in the Development of Nigeria*, (ed) I.A.B Balogun, P A Dopamu et.al (Ilorin: Department of Religions, University of Ilorin(Unilorin),1988); J.A Ayoade, "Concept of Inner Essence in Yoruba Traditional Medicine," in *African Therapeutic System*, ed. Z.A. Admuwagun et.al. (Massechussett: Cross Road Press, 1979); Dr. J Ubrurhe, "Urhobo Traditional Medicine," A PhD Thesis, UNN, Nigeria, 1993. I am indebted to Dr. J.O Ubrurhe, who is my colleague at Delta State University, Abraka, for some of these ideas.

[9] Many African scholars have vehemently condemned these foreigners' description of

20

African medicine. I think that African scholars should learn to understand the complexity of the foreigners situation. What they tried to do is to judge African indigenous medicine by their western experience without taking into consideration the African peculiar situation and culture.

[10]L. Keita, "The African Philosophical Tradition," *in African Philosophy* ed. Richard Wright, (Lanham MD:University Press of America, 1984), 8.

[11]Check Anta Diop, *Africa in Antiquity*, Egypt is part of Africa, not Europe as some western scholars tried to make us believe. The majority of the ancient Pharaohs are black, except the Pharaoh of the Hyksos peoriod, who were eventually driven away from Egypt. A closer look at the sculpture of Akhinaton, Queen Tiye, Hatseptsut, Tirhaqar would reveal the black characteristics feautures.

[12] Second College Edition, David B Guralnik,ed.,(New York: Simon and Schuster, 1980), 882.

[13]"Health and Healing ," 67

[14]J.O Mume, "Traditional Medicine in Nigeria," 27.

[15]A Sofowora, *Medicinal Plants and Traditional Medicine in Africa*, (Ibadan:Spectrum Books, 1984),21.

[16]E.I Metuh, "African Taditional Medicine and Healing: A Theological Pastoral Appraisal," *Lucerna* (Jan-June 1985), 5.

[17]"The Theology of Medicine," *Journal of African Religion aamd Philosophy*(JARP) vol .2 ,no 1, (1991),23-33.

[18] The early missionaries, anthropologists and travellers to Africa used this word magic to mean "clever trickery." They call it a jumble of deceitful acts as evident in the work of the magicians who have perfected their tricks. Some early Western investigators witnessed some African medicien men who performed their healing and other wel-being medicine and could not underst how the do their work mainly because of the secrecy involved. They therefore tag them as magicians. They were also called liars and deceitful people when they

Endnotes

witnessed some of the unsuccessful medicine men. Instead of magic, I would prefer the

word, "mystery medicine."

[19]Ibid.

[20]However, this is not to say that there are no Africans who parade themselves as medicine-men but are deceivers. There are as many as those fake western medical doctors who parade themselves as qualified medical doctors. The fact is that the Yoruba people differentiate between medicine and magic. *Oogun* or *eegbogi* is medicine while *idan* is magic. The word *apidan* means a magician. The words are never used interchangeably. *Idon* is a skill trickery. A magician in the Yoruba sense is the person who entertains by the use of artful trick. Although a medicine man or woman may possess the knowledge of medicine and the art of trickery, all medicine persons do not possess the art.

[21]The story was narrated on the radio programme called *Irri Aaye* that comes up every Saturday at Ibadan, Nigeria.This story was also verified by the producer of the programme.

[22]*The Sacred Power in Your Name* (St. Paul, Minnesota: Llewellyn Publications, 1990), xi.

[23]Ibid. xii

CHAPTER III

Survey of African Indigenous Churches

African indigenous Churches have been given so many names such as Aladura Churches (Praying Churches), Pentecostal Churches, African Independence Churches, Zionist Churches, White Garment Churches, Ethiopian Churches and others. Aladura Churches is Yoruba in Origin (*Ijo Aladura*). It is given to them because of their emphasis on the power of prayer. The name Pentecostal Churches was given to them by some western people because the way they pray, their emphasis on the spirit and the way they read and interpret the Bible is Pentecostal in nature. They called them African Independent Churches because they claim to be independent from western and the mainline churches' control. They also gave them Protest Churches because of the belief that they walked out of the western mainline churches in Africa as a protest against unAfrican Christian type of worship. The name Zionist was given because of their Pentecostal nature of praying in spirit and healing. The name White Garment is given to them simply because they wear white robes that is believed to be what the angels wear in heaven. They called them Ethiopian Churches because their establishment is political in nature. Even though they are independent, they still retain the worship pattern of the mainline churches from where they separated.

The formation of African Indigenous churches is a result of a process of ecclesiastical experimentation that started in the face of much opposition. The static nature of the so-called mainline churches toward change contrasts badly over against the dynamic adaptability of the AIC. This adaptability is seen in their liturgy, choruses, and ritual innovations, their emphasis on special methods of sharing, and caring, in situation of rapid social change, their method of healing, money saving, and money lending in situations of deprivation.

There are many churches in Nigeria so much so that almost every street has a church. It is important that my readers understand the type of churches referred to as African Indigenous churches in Nigeria. These churches has been labeled many kinds of names such as separatist, Ethiopian, Zionist, Spiritual, Prophetic, *Aladura* (Praying) churches, Pentecostal churches, African Independent churches, White Garment Churches, Schismatic Churches and others. I would like to examine these names and the reason why I deliberately chose the name African Indigenous churches. These terms are used interchangeably most of the time.

African Indigenous Churches in Nigeria.

Some of my readers may be wondering who the African Indigenous Churches are and whose practices of interpretation we are discussing. It is then important to discuss briefly few of the Nigerian African Indigenous Churches that I know well and visited throughout my research period. I intentionally limited my discussion to the history of the few of the indigenous churches in Nigeria. It is impossible for me to discuss all of them in West Africa, East, Central, and South Africa. One of the major reasons is that the history of these indigenous churches has been written over and over again in this continent.[1] In this survey, I would like to discuss the history of Cherubim and Seraphim, Christ Apostolic Church, Celestial Church of Christ, and The Church of the Lord: Aladura which originated in Nigeria as representative of all the indigenous churches in Africa.

Christ Apostolic Church

The founder of Christ Apostolic Church in Nigeria is Joseph Ayo Babalola, a native of Odo Owa, Ilofa , Kwara State, Nigeria where he was born in 1904. He attended Anglican Primary School, Osogbo, Osun State, Nigeria. He worked as a dispensary aid in a private hospital. He later became a motor mechanic. He worked in the Public Works Department in 1928 as a steamroller operator at Igbara–Oke construction. The same year he began to have strange dreams and all kinds of experiences. Even though he interpreted all the strange experiences as a sign of God's call to the ministry as an evangelist, he refused that call for several months until October, 1928 when all of a sudden his steamroller failed to function.[2] He interpreted this experience as an act of God because of his disobedience of God's call. Hence, he quit his job for God's call as a missionary. In his dream he heard the voice that prayer and water *(omi iye)* would be enough to heal all kinds of diseases and infirmities. Babalola took his Bible and a large school bell in his town and began the work of evangelist. He organized a prayer meeting and Bible study in the local Anglican Church in his hometown from where he was later excommunicated. He continued his missionary work in one of the lay reader's house (Elder Olayemi). Elder Olayemi was also excommunicated from the local Anglican Church.[3] Because of much opposition, Babalola left his home town, Odo-Owa, for Ibadan and Lagos where he met Pastor Odubanjo who was a Faith Tabernacle church member. He was later rebaptized and joined Faith Tabernacle Church in Lagos.

Revival at Ilesha

At a meeting in Ilesha, where Babalola was a delegate, Odubanjo introduced him as a man full of the Holy Spirit. One day Babalola raised a dead child who was on the way to the cemetery to be buried.

That led to a great revival in Ilesha. The miracle gave him the opportunity to preach to the people at that meeting and others. He asked his listeners to forsake witchcraft and all evil practices. Many people were also healed. This miracle brought many people from the nearby towns to Ilesha and Evangelist Babalola consecrated a river (Oye river) near the revival ground for healing all kinds of diseases. Many people from their hospital beds were also taken to the evangelist and he healed them. For this sake, the District Officer at Ilesha had to intervene charging the evangelist for disrupting the hospital services. However, there was a successful great revival at Ilesha.

The Evangelist went to another revival meeting at Ondo State at Efon Alaye. He continued to accuse people of witchcraft and sorcery. Because of his consecration of water for healing and advice to abandon hospital, the Faith tabernacle leaders were accused of inciting the people against the government. Babalola himself was accused of forcing people to take unhygienic water (*omi iye*) and calling the government hospital a satanic institution. In Ilesha, some of the leaders of Faith Tabernacle church were arrested and detained for the activities of Evangelist Babalola. The government eventually banned the consecration of water, witch hunting, challenge of other cults, condemnation of other religious faiths, keeping neighborhood awake by vigils, and the organized open or public revival meetings.

When the Evangelist was conducting a meeting at Benin, Edo State, he was picked up and jailed for six months in a town in Afemai Division. As a result of this great persecution, Faith Tabernacle was affiliated with another apostolic church in Bradford, Great Britain as a way of seeking external assistance. This affiliation with British Apostolic church made the Nigerian Faith Tabernacle to adopt the name Apostolic Church, and some missionaries of the British Apostolic church were sent to Nigeria. They made personal contacts with the British Government authorities and the persecution was relaxed. Hence, Evangelist

Babalola was released from prison to continue his missionary work and he established new Assemblies, schools and apostolic churches.

Nigerian Apostolic Church

In less than ten years of the affiliation, tension arose when the key members of the apostolic church who were Nigerians discovered that the missionaries of the British Apostolic Church were taking medicine (quinine) for malaria. Despite all the explanation of the missionaries that there was nothing wrong in taking curative and preventive medicine, Nigerian leaders refused to accept such explanation and expressed shock and great disappointment. The discovery was made known to the public and in 1939 most of the Nigerian Apostolic members broke away to form Nigerian Apostolic Church. Few others who were sympathetic with the missionaries remained with them and named their church, The Apostolic Church.

Later, the name Nigerian Apostolic Church was dropped when the church spread beyond Nigeria. They adopted United Apostolic Church UAC) to express their unity with other churches in other countries such as Ghana in 1940. It was realized that this abbreviation (UAC) correspond with a famous commercial firm in Nigeria, therefore, he name was dropped and Christ Apostolic Church was adopted in 1941. This name was believed to be divinely revealed and was registered in 1943. There was an emphasis on the efficacy of Prayer, fasting, and divine healing. Although they accepted the use of oil and water for anointing and healing purposes, they rejected indigenous and Western orthodox medicine. This belief is very strong and was included in their constitution: "Divine healing through obedience to the command of our Lord Jesus Christ; Faith in His Name and Merit of His Blood for all sickness, diseases and infirmities."[4] They believe in Monogamous marriage and Existence of Sacred Hills endorsed. Article IX of the CAC tenets on the government list the key leaders as Apostles, Prophets, Evangelists, Pastors, Teachers, Elders, and Deacons.

Christ Apostolic Church has established branches in Britain and United States. Most of the members of the church are African immigrant and non-immigrants.

Cherubim and Seraphim Churches

This is one of the most prominent African Indigenous Churches in Nigeria. They are very active and aggressive in the practice of their religion in a way that is indigenous to the people of Africa, particularly, the Yoruba of Nigeria. Although there is a firm belief among the members that this church is not founded by human being, there is a historical fact that it started as a prayer group in Lagos in 1925 under the able leadership of Moses Orimolade Tunolase.

The Prophet Orimolade

The prophet Orimolade was born in Ikare Akoko, Ondo State, Nigeria in 1870s with a crippled leg. All of a sudden he had a vision to go to a stream to use its water for the purpose of healing. He obeyed and was partially healed. Soon after this miracle he became a traveling evangelist-preacher. Between 1916-1924 he traveled to many parts of Yoruba land, Midwestern, and Northern Nigeria. Wherever he went, miracles were performed through his preaching. Although he did not obtain western education, people were fascinated by the way he quoted Bible passages from memory. The prophet was immensely successful in Ilorin, Kwara State, Nigeria, although he was not allowed to establish a church there because of the strong Muslim presence. At Ilorin, he was named Alhaji Yisa (the Muslim name for Jesus). He eventually moved to Ibadan where he continued his prayer meetings. In 1924 he traveled to Lagos where his popularity increased as a miracle worker. There he was called *Baba Aladura* (The praying Father).

When his style of preaching and prayer came under severe criticism in Lagos among the members of the Holy Trinity Church, he visited homes, prayed for, and preached to the people. He continued his evangelistic ministry without any objective of establishing a church until he met a teen-age girl call *Abiodun Akinsowon.*

Praying Society

On the 18th of June 1925, Miss. Abiodun Christianah Akinsowon at the age of fifteen went to Catholic Corpus Christi procession in company of her friends. She saw a strange spectacle that is an angel of the Lord, under the Corpus Christi canopy. As a result she became feverish and was taken home where she fell into a trance. This trance continued for many days. When Rev. T.A Ogunbiyi, the vicar of the church was invited to revive her, he could not. But the prophet Orimolade came and prayed for her and she came out of her trance and recounted the mysterious things that happened to her when she was in the celestial city. Many people came to Miss Abiodun's house where she served as a ward to Mr. and Mrs. Hunny Moiett. Mr. and Mrs. Hunny became embarrassed and therefore, they asked Abiodun to follow the prophet for full recovery. Many other people started going to the Prophet's house to listen to Abiodun's story. The prophet Orimolade took advantage of this and started a prayer society in his house.

The Origin of the Name Cherubim and Seraphim

As the society grew fast, there was a need to give it a specific name. The prophet proclaimed a fast and prayer for the revelation of the name of the society. On September 9th 1925, one member of the society claimed to have seen a name written in fire on the sky, the letters SE. It was then interpreted that the SE is the beginning of the word *SERAFU* (Seraph). The society therefore accepted this interpretation given by one of the associate member of the society. The name then became *Egbe Sarafu* (Cherubim Society) and it was incorporated. However, another woman came up to say that it was wrong for that name to stand alone without the name Cherubim. Consequently, the members embraced the name Cherubim and Seraphim society.

After the revelation of his name and the acceptance by the society, they decided to elect a patron. Archangel Michael was elected as the Patron or Captain, and Angel Gabriel its Deputy- patron. This election is to seal a unique relationship with the heavenly host because the society already existed in heaven before the establishment of the society. The Prophet Orimolade commanded the society to wear white robes to imitate the Cherubim and Seraphim who are believed to array in white

robes in heaven. With aggressive evangelism the society spread far and wide to Agege, Abeokuta, Ondo, Ijebu-Ode, and Ibadan, Nigeria.[5]

Division in Cherubim and Seraphim Society

In less than four years after the inception of the society, symptoms of conflict between the prophet Orimolade and Christiana Abiodun began. All attempt to smother the conflict failed. A clique of youth who called themselves the valiant 12 were on the side of Abiodun and continued to flattered her that she was more popular than the prophet Orimolade. They encouraged the break up. The first secession by the prophet was in 1929. At this time Orimolade asked for the intervention of the police. Eventually Orimolade wrote a letter to Miss Abiodun that

..I am therefore asking you through this letter to inform you to form your own society taking with youall the members as are willing to follow and cooperate with you..[6]

Abiodun created her own faction retaining the name Cherubim and Seraphim Society, while Orimolade faction adopted the name The Eternal Sacred Order of Cherubim and Seraphim Society. The second secession was another disagreement between Orimolade and the Praying Band within his own society in 1930. A section of the Prayer Band tried to rob Orimolade of the leadership of the society. Under the leadership of Ezekiel Davies, a group in the Prayer Band seceded and called themselves "The Prayng Band of C & S." The prophet's court injunction did not stop this group from seceding. Another secession was when the leaders of the branches in the Western part of the country appealed for an end to the secession. They registered their displeasure by inaugurating their own separate organization called "The Western Conference of the C & S (Nigeria)" under the leadership of Madam Christianah Olatunde who later became the General Superintendent.

The fourth secession was in 1932 with the announcement of Major A. Lawrence, one of the leaders of the Praying Band. He announced that he had a vision to establish his own organization called the Holy Flock of Christ Church. Yet another secession came immediately after the death of the prophet Orimolade in 1933. Apparently the prophet had appointed one Mr. Onanuga, a latecomer, but a gifted prophet, as his successor over and above another prospective person, Mr. Peter Omojola, who was Orimolade's own elder brother. A group who felt that Mr. Onanuga was not qualified to be the successor encouraged Omojola to form his own church. He did and named it "Eternal Sacred Order of the C & s (Mount Zion)." The secession continued until today as described by Onovughakpo:

Founding one's own branch and headquarters is as simple as winking the eye. The procedure is first to procure for yourself the power of vision and prophecy. The next step is to approach an Apostle or Bishop to revive the Order of Apostleship. As you settle down in a neighboring or far away town your parlor becomes the Cathedra Church and your room the headquarters... Your house becomes consulting chamber for all sorts of people: boys and girls anxious about love , students wishing to pass their examinations, clerks and executive officers seeking promotion and the poor and destitute seeking wealth..[7]

This society later became the societies with more

splinter groups than any other in Nigeria. There are so many of them scattered all over the world, each claiming to be the headquarters of the society. However, despite the divisions, they seem to adhere to the same beliefs and practices. Their belief in expressing the Africanness of Christianity is uniformly strong. Their forms of prayer which include reading Psalms a number of times, and calling on the name of God certain number of times. They believe in polygamous marriage as is the custom of African indigenous tradition, in Spiritual agencies, using African traditional instrument for their music, and traditional language in worship. They strongly believe in interpretation of visions, dreams, trances and tongues. The prophets and elders, called "Alagba," occupy a great position of honor with the usual Yoruba traditional greetings of kneeling down.[8]

The Church of the Lord (Aladura)

Ifakoya Dawodu Oshitelu (Founder)

Oshitelu was born at Ogere in 1902. He renounced his first two names at his baptism and took the name Josiah Oluwalowo. At a young age he was zealous for the Lord in the Anglican Church at Ogere. After his elementary education he continued in the service of the Lord in the Anglican Church as a teacher and catechist. As Oshitelu was preparing to go to St. Andrews College in Oyo to become a trained teacher, he started having strange visionary experiences that he could not understand. His investigation led him to an older Prophet Somoye who explained to him that the visionary experiences meant a call to be a prophet. He warned him to stop the use of traditional medicine, put his faith on God, read psalms for his daily devotion and fast. He followed the instruction of the Prophet Somoye and started prayer and fasting. As he continued this practice, he claimed to have heard the voice of God confirming what Prophet Somoye had predicted for him. As he continued in this spiritual development, he was noticed by some Elders of Anglican Churche who warned him to desist from such unorthodox practices. When Oshitelu refused, he was excomunicated from the Anglican Church. He then proceeded to Prophet Somoye and became his apprentice for several years. In 1929 he emerged as a prophetic teacher, and organized his first revival in his hometown on June 9th. He inaugurated his church the following year, July 1930 at Ogere.

Expansion of the Ministry

His fame spread quickly like other leaders of indigenous churches such as Babalola, Abiodun, Orimolade. The Faith Tabernacle church was interested in his evangelistic ministry but because of his use of strange names and the so-called "sealed words," the two could not agree. Prophet Oshitelu claimed that special names of God were revealed to him. Such names are *AWOBISLILLAL* (Healer), *ARRABABLALHUS, ANOMOLNOMOLLAHHUJAH*. He insisted that these names were revealed to him in accordance with Ezekiel 33:7, "So will I make my holy name known in the midst of my people..."
The church and the disciples embarked on mass evangelistic campaigns, the result of which is church growth and expansion of the church to the towns of Oyo and Ijebu, Ondo, and Ekiti. A very gifted evangelist, Mr. Adeleke Adejobi also joined the church and became Oshitelu's disciple. In 1940, this able evangelist opened a church in Lagos where Oshitelu had not been able to establish the church.

In 1945, Primate Oshitelu had a vision of the church's expansion beyond Nigeria. He, therefore, commissioned Apostles Adejobi and Oduwole to establish the church outside Nigeria. While Adejobi went to Sierra Leone, Oduwole went to countries. Adejobi also established the church in Glasgow while he was on a two-year Bible training course. The church has spread all over the world including the United States of America.

The belief of the Church of the Lord include special prayer and fasting with the elaborate use of the book of Psalms., revelations, the use of sacred objects, special healing technique, celebration of an annual festival called Taborah, and polygamy. Worship services are elaborate. It includes thanksgiving with shouts of "Halleluyah, Hosanna," with the outburst of laughter, jumping, prostrating, and singing before the Lord. The church uses holy rosary, vestments, small and handy crosses, candles, palm leaves, and other symbolic objects. To enter the church all shoes must be removed.

Celestial Church of Christ (CCC)

Celestial Church of Christ is one of the most attractive and flourishing indigenous churches in Africa today. It is a relatively young organization established in 1947.

Pastor S.B.J Oshoffa (Founder).

Mr. Samuel Bilewu (Bileou) Joseph Oshoffa was born in a small village near Port-Novo, Dahomey (Benin) on May 18, 1909. During his infancy his father arranged for him to live with a Methodist Bishop of Port Novo, David Hodonu Loco. Oshoffa attended his elementary school in a Methodist Primary School but was not allowed to attend a seminary because he refused to make blocks for their hostels. As a result he was forced to learn carpentry, his father's profession.

God called Pastor Oshoffa in May 1947 when he was lost in the forest for three months and lived on honey and water. At that time he had time for fervent prayers. Immediately when he came out of the forest, he claimed he had the revelation that God had appointed him a worldwide evangelist to preach the Gospel of Jesus Christ. As part of the assurance of this call, he healed a young man (Kudiho) who was sick by laying his hand on his dead body. As a result of this miracle many people around came to Oshoffa's house where Kudiho resided. Pastor Oshoffa performed many more miracles that baffled the people. At Porto Novo, He healed and brought to life his nephew who had died earlier. He continued to heal many people at Porto-Novo. The event that actually confirmed his call into the ministry happened on September 29, 1947 when Oshoffa saw a vision of a ray of light, and an angel assured him of his call to the ministry. Moreover, one of the members of his praying bands fell into a trance and confirmed Oshoffa's call to the ministry.[9]

The Birth and Spread of Celestial Church of Christ

After the above miracle, Pastor Oshoffa continued to have visions and the hearing of God's voices telling him the type of a church he should establish. One of his members was in a trance for seven days and came out with this message written on the wall of Oshoffa's house: *Eglise Du Christianisme Celeste(Yoruba: Ijo mimo ti ti Kkristi lat Orun wa)*. The meaning of this writing is Holy Assembly of Christ from Heaven. This became the beginning of the identification of this prayer group with the name of Celestial Church of Christ.

The church spread rapidly to Nigeria and other parts of the world. Persecution forced Oshoffa to shift his base from Porto-Novo to Nigeria beause of persecution from the government of President Kerekou. Kerekou ordered all institutions (including the churches) to declare their properties. Oshoffa expressed his disgust for such order. Third, many members of the mainline missionary churches defected to Celestial Church of Christ.

He moved to Lagos, Nigeria, where he thought he could be saved because some fishermen from Benin had already introduced this church to Lagos. Oshoffa arrived in Lagos in 1951 and continued his ministry with numerous miracles. The church spread rapidly and registered on November 24th, 1958 in Nigeria. In 1977, it established his international headquarters at Ketu, near

Lagos.   Before the death of Oshoffa on September 10, 1985, the church had about 1600 branches all over the world. This makes it one of the fastest growing churches in the world.

Members follow a set of worship services. During worship services, there is what is called *AMISSA,* that is, invocation of the soul of the dead performed once a year. At the entrance of the church members dip their fingers in a concentrated water to make sign of the cross. Members prostrate at the entrance of the church and touch the floor of the church with their foreheads before the service starts with the lighting of seven candles. Fasting is limited but it is not forbidden. Sometimes the members are called the "barefooted celestial" because members are not allowed to wear any kind of footwear around the church or whenever they are wearing their gowns, called "sutana."

Women had to be purified after menstruation and childbirth because they are regarded as unclean. A prophet can occasionally order any member in need to be in a confinement for safety (*abe abo* in Yoruba). Naming ceremony can be very elaborate and the prophets have the responsibility of giving names to newborn babies during a naming ceremony. It is a taboo for any woman to reach or sit at the altar. No red or black clothing should be worn, especially on top of their white robe. "Green water" is provided for the sick to drink for healing. In the church or around the church there is a place called "Mercy-land" where special prayers could be offered. Sea sand and usually a well are provided to make the place a sacred ground.[10]

Characteristics of African Indigenous Churches

Having discussed very briefly, each of these churches, I feel it is important to bring out the characteristics of these indigenous churches.   I believe they are uniform. Of course, with few exceptions, these characteristics are probably true of all African indigenous churches.

Emphasis on African-worldview

The most prominent and widest characteristic of African indigenous churches is the strong interest in the use of African worldview in their mode of reading and interpreting the Bible. This actually distinguish African Christianity from the western Christianity. The missionary/western ways of reading and interpreting the Bible is too foreign to meet the urgent needs of Africans. They are down-to- earth in their belief, doctrine, and response to the problems of their African congregation. These indigenous churches preach the message that is rooted in African culture and in light of the existence of evil spirits, witches and wizard, dreams, trances and visions. They respond to these problems through exorcism, rituals, sacrifices, prayers, fasting, bathing, and the power of words.

Divine Healing

There is a strong and universal belief in divine healing among the African indigenous churches. In Africa, where hospitals and orthodox medicine are beyond the reach of so many Africans, one would expect that the promise of special healing by the Almighty God would attract visitors. In fact, the most pungent reason given for becoming members of African indigenous churches is *cura divina*. Special days (usually Wednesday and Friday) are set up for healing purposes. There are series of testimonies about miracles that have been performed by God through these churches. Most of them claim that these healings take place after the failure of the hospitals and traditional healers. Most of those who are healed remain as members of these churches. Sometimes, spiritual or faith healing homes that serve as clinics are set up adjacent to the churches for the sick and pregnant women.

Prayer

This is also wide spread in all the African indigenous churches all over Africa. No wonder the Yoruba people of Nigeria refer to these churches as *Aladura* (praying people). The leaders are also referred to as prayer father (*Baba Aladura*) and praying mothers (*Iya Aladura*). There are always prayer group called praying warrior (*A f'adura Jagun*-Yoruba), *Mpaec-Kuo* (Akan In Ghana). Their major responsibilities in the churches are to pray and fast for the needy, the sick, and special programs of the churches. Special places are designated for prayer places such as mercy land, beaches, Garden, and other places. They firmly believed that their prayers could be heard from these places more than anywhere else. Most of them use special prayer aids such as candles, the book of Psalms, incense, and palm fronts and special books with the list of the holy names of God to be pronounced repeatedly.

Spirituality

There is an emphasis on the spiritual. As mentioned earlier, many of these churches prefer to be called spiritual churches (*Ijo Emi*-Yoruba, *Sunsuni*-Akan, *Momo sulemo*-Ga, *Ishoshi rerhi*-Urhobo, *Uka onso* Nsuko-Igbo). By this they claimed to be filled and directed by the Holy Spirit in their activities. The purpose of establishment of the churches is always spiritual. Spiritual interpretation is given to all events, especially misfortunes such as sicknesses, unemployment, disappointments, poverty, bareness and others. Special spiritual solutions are, therefore, prescribed for these problems. That is why faith healing services, exorcism are constantly part of the activities of the church. The Holy Spirit is prominent as manifested in their interpretation of visions, dreams, ecstatic behavior, and prophetic utterances. The members are advised to wear white gowns because it is a sign of the holiness and purity, which the Holy Spirit prefers.

Evangelism and Revival

There is an unusual enthusiasm for evangelism and revival among these indigenous churches. Most of their leaders are itinerary preachers who go from one place to another preaching revival. This is very true of Joseph Babalola of Christ Apostolic Church, Moses Orimolade of Cherubim and Seraphim Church, Oshitelu of The Church of the Lord (Aladura), and Oshoffa of Celestial Church of Christ, and others all around Africa. Ordinary members are always advised to lead about seven to twenty revival or open-air revival crusades outside the church. This led to the rapid growth of these churches.

Flexible Worship Services

Africans are action-oriented people. They enjoy flexible and demonstrative form of worship rather than the dull Eurocentric liturgy of the mission churches. Everyone has an opportunity to participate in spirit and soul. African indigenous churches have made African participants feel more at home with the chanting, clapping, singing, dancing and stamping of feet. Most of the time such activity is absent in the mainline missionary churches. Every one is inspired to pray, to deliver a message, to sing and give testimony. Most of the songs take the form of indigenous lyrics, with invocations, spontaneous composition and responsorial type of songs. The use of native musical instrument such as bell, drums and others are always attractive to the members and non-members who attend the worship services.

Elaborate Role of Women

One of the distinctive characteristics of these churches is the important elevated position given to women. Unlike the mission churches, who preach equality of sexes, and yet make men hold mostly all the principal position of authority in their churches. The position of Archbishops, ministers, pastors, Priests, choir masters and so on could be held by women in African indigenous churches. It is not unusual to have prophetesses and deaconesses, Reverend Mothers, Lady Leaders, Mothers in Israel, Superior Mothers. Praying mothers, Lay Evangelist, Women church planters, and other leadership names in African indigenous churches. In these churches, women are more possessed, they prophesy, they dance, they sing, clap, and give more testimonies than men. They are always in the majority and are more active. In fact they are church founders.[11]

Emphasis on the Power of Words

One of the major characteristics of these churches is the belief in potent words spoken by the prophets and apostles, or the words read and recited from the Bible. There is an emphasis on the memorization of the words of God and the repetitive pronunciation of certain words for effectiveness. Members are instructed to learn to say those words not only repeatedly, but also at certain times and certain places for their potency. The background of this practice is African culture and religion where words are regarded as potent if repeated and said at certain time and places, mostly at the middle of the night. The word of God may be prescribed to be read seven times during midnight and while naked (more will be said about this later).

Power in Names

Like the African indigenous religion and culture, a strong belief in the power in names dominates these churches. They claim that special names of God are revealed to them to heal, to bring success in life, and to protect against all evil forces. Members are encouraged to repeat God's names as part of their prayers. Booklets containing the revealed names of God are printed for members and the general public. There is no doubt whatsoever that those names are potent. Most of the names include names of God in the Hebrew Bible. More will be discussed in later chapter on names.

Endnotes

[1] Any one interested in the history of these indigenous churches can consult the following documents: Harold W. Turner, History of an African Independent

Church , Vol. 1&2 (London: Claredon Press, 1967); Victor Hayward, ed. *African Independent Church Movements: Essays in Honour of Harold W.Turner,* (Elkhart: Mission Focusl Publications, 1990); J.D Y Peel, *Aladura: A Religious Movement among the Yoruba* (London: OUP., 1964); J.A Omoyajowo, *Cherubim and Seraphim: The History of an African Indepenednt Church Church* (New York: Nok, 1982); O .Oshun, "Christ Apostolic Church of Nigeria: A Penteostal Consideration of its Historical, Theological and Organisational Developments 1918-1978," PhD Thesis, Exeter, 1981. Ogbu Kalu, ed. *Chirstianity in West Africa: The Nigerian Story* (Ibadan: Daystar Press, 1978); David Barret, *Schism and Renewal in Africa* (London: OUP., 1968); M L Daneel, *Zionsism and Faith-Healing in Rhodesia: Aspects of African Independent Churches* (Leiden: Africa_Studiecentrum, 1970); G. M Bengt Sundkler, *Bantu Prophcts in South Africa* (London: OUP., 1961); S.A Adewale, *The African Church Inc., 1901-1986* (Ibadan: n.p 1988).

[2] A.F Walls, African Independent Churches," in Tim Dowley, et al (eds.) *Edmans Handbook of the History of Christianity* (Grand Rapids: Eerdmans, 1977), 27

[3] Ishola and Aiyegboyin, *African Indigenous Churches: An Historical Perspective* (Lagos: Greater Heights Publications, 1997), 73

[4] *CHRIST APOSTOLIC CHURCH Official Magazine of CAC.* Vol. 25:1 (May 1992), 6

[5] J.D Y Peel, "The Aladura Movement in Western Nigeria," in *Tariqh*, Vol. 3:1 (1969), 47ff.

[6] Omoyajowo, *Diversity in Unity: The Develoment and Espansion of the C & S Church in Nigeria* (Lanham:University Press of America, 1982), 65

Endnotes

[7] G.C Onovughakpo, History and Doctine of the Cherubim and Seraphim Church

(Warri: Midland Press, 1971

[8] Ishola and Aiyegboyin, *African Indigenous Churches*, 88.

[9] Ibid., 99

[10] For further details of the belief of the Celetial, see Ishola and Aiyegboyin, Rev. Yemi Soetan, *The Hidden Secrets about Celestial Church of Christ* (Abeokuta, Nigeria: Lifeline World Outreach, 1995).

[11] See J. A Omoyajowo, "The Aladura Chuches in Nigeria since Independence," in Fashole-Luke et al (eds) *Christianity in Independence Africa* (Ibadan: Oxford University Press, 1978) for a list of women founders of churches in Nigeria.

CHAPTER IV

African Cultural Hermeneutics

This section is also crucial to the understanding of the rest of the chapters. It enables us to understanding the relationship between culture, the Bible and Christianity. It gives the exact definition of what I mean by African cultural hermeneutics. Let me state categorically that African culture, Bible, and Christian faith are not identical. Culture is the context in which individuals are socialized.[1] It shapes our worldview. Deotis Roberts is right concerning his statement about culture.

> Culture is intergenerational, sustaining values that parents share with their children. Many intellectual and literary devices are used to pass from one generation to another the knowledge of life born of experience. Mythology, folklore, stories, poetry, and many other means of communication are used to pass cultural traits down through history. All people including Africans and African Americans, have a culture.[2]

The fact is that God created culture for human well-being. God created human being with the ability and the need for culture. Culture is not inherently evil or good. There is no perfect culture anywhere. It is something to be used by human beings and God. Culture could be influenced by human sin. Culture is the milleu by which there may be an encounter between God and humankind. Deotis continues to see culture as

> "an integrated pattern of human knowledge, belief, and behavior that depens upon human capacities to learn and pass on these traits to future generations. Culture may be said to be a set of customary beliefs, social

forms, and material traits of a particular ethnic, racial, religious, or social groups.[3]

No one can escape from culture even though we may be able to transform, replace, and improve on it. Culture is important to biblical studies but cannot replace biblical studies. The revelation of God is universal. Human explanation of divine revelation is conditioned by culture. Our interpretation of the Bible can be affected by our culture. What you are about to read below is the example of how African indigenous Churches have made good use of culture in their interpretation of the Bible and Christianity. Before I discuss these examples, let me share what I mean by African cultural Hermeneutics.

Definition of African Cultural Hermeneutics[4]

African cultural hermeneutic in biblical studies is an approach to biblical interpretation that makes African social cultural context a subject of interpretation.[5] It means that African cultural hermeneutic, like any other Third World hermeneutic, is contextual hermeneutics since interpretation is always done in a particular context. Specifically it means that analysis of the text is done from the perspective of African world-view and culture.[6] African cultural hermeneutics is rereading the scripture from a premeditatedly Africentric perspective. The purpose is not only to understand the Bible and God in our African experience and culture, but also with the hope to break the hermeneutical hegemony and ideological stranglehold that Eurocentric biblical scholars have long enjoyed.[7] This is a methodology that reappraises ancient biblical tradition and African world-view, culture, and life experience with the purpose of "correcting the effect of the cultural ideological conditioning to which Africa and Africans have been subjected."

Conditions for African Cultural Hermeneutics

In order to do African cultural hermeneutics successfully, some conditions are important and should be mentioned as a guide:

The interpreter must be an insider. This means that the would- be interpreter must be either an African or someone who live and experience all aspects of African life in Africa. By this it is difficult to do African cultural hermeneutic without living in Africa and going through, the joys, problems of poverty, ethnicity, hunger, communalism and other palatable and unpalatable aspects of African culture.

He or she must be immersed in the content of the Bible. It is not enough just to know the content, it is absolutely necessary to believe the stories and the event of the Bible as a life of faith. In other words, the biblical events are reflections of our own present individual and communal life. The interpreter must be a person of faith. There must be a firm belief in the power of God's word.

3   Understanding African indigenous culture is absolutely important in doing African cultural hermeneutics. This is because African culture is part and parcel of African cultural hermeneutics. Despite the resemblance of the biblical and African cultures, there are still some distinct aspects of African culture. This distinctive African culture influences or dominates the interpretation of the Bible.

Faith in God who is all-powerful is an important condition for African cultural hermeneutic. This faith in God is not only in his existence but also in his absolute power to do and undo. He is in control and he performs miracles at will. This God can use any means to heal, protect, and bring success in all life endeavor.

Ability to read or memorize the words of the Bible is important.

The interpreter may not necessarily be a scholar of the Bible. Some of the evangelists in Africa are illiterate, yet they use the word of God to perform miracles and wonders in Africa. Some blind evangelists have good memories to memorize the Bible. They have also used the words of God to achieve great things in Africa.[8]

Endnotes

[1] J. Deotis Roberts, *Africentrism*, 69

[2] Ibid., 71

[3] Ibid., 79

[4] Part of this section was taken from my article, "African Cultural Hermeneutics," in *Vernacular Hermeneutics* (Sheffield: Sheffield Academic Press, 1999), 66-90

[5] Ibid.,5

[6] ibid., 6

[7] This is what Yorke calls "Afrocentic hermeneutic" which is very legitmate since all interpretations and theologies are perspectival. Gosnell L. Yorke, "Biblical Hermeneutics:an Afrocentric Perspective,"*Journal of Religion and Theology*, vol 2, no 2(1995), 145-158.

[8] David Adamo, "African Cultural Hermeneutics," in Vernacular Hermeneutics, (Sheffield: Sheffield Academic Press, 1999)

CHAPTER V

Reading and Interpreting the Bible Therapeutically

In the African indigenous culture, the means of dealing with traditional problems like diseases, sorcerers, witches, enemies, and lack of success in life experience, have been developed. Western missionaries taught African Christians to discard these indigenous ways of handling these problems without offering any concrete alternative. Charms, medicine, incantations, divination, sacrifices and other cultural ways of protecting, healing, and liberating from the evil powers in African forests were hurriedly discarded in the name of Christianity. Yet, we were not taught how to use the Bible as a means of protecting, healing, and solving the daily problems of life. The Euro-American way of reading the Bible has not actually helped us to understand the Bible in our own context.[1]

Faced with some peculiar problems as African Christians, we search the Bible consistently with our own eyes in order to discover whether there could be anything in the Bible that can solve our problems. In the process of reading the Bible in our own eyes, we discovered in the scripture great affinities with our own worldview and culture. We discovered in both the Old and New Testaments, resemblance to events similar to the African experience, especially painful experiences. Examples of these activities are miracles, encounters with satanic powers, the reality of hunger, and the deliverance of the oppressed. In the miracles that were narrated in the Bible, many means of healing were used.

These include medicine, pronouncement of words, touching, prayers, and ordinary water. We then started asking questions as to how to read and interpret the Bible with "our own eyes" to meet our daily needs as African Christians. What follows is how Africans read and interpret the Bible for therapeutic purposes.

African Indigenous Therapeutic System

Healing in African Culture

Healing in African Indigenous culture is a corporate matter. It involves the totality of the individual person, the family and the community. This is what I may call the concept of corporate responsibility in African health system. Good health in African indigenous concept differs remarkably from the Western concept. Unlike the World Health Organization (WHO) which defines good health as the absence of disease or infirmity, African concept has to do with the state of total physical, mental, social-well being as a result of maintenance of good relationship and harmony with nature, divinities, spirits and fellow being.[2] Health, therefore, involves the physical, psychosocial, spiritual, and environmental. In African context, lack of good health or diseases can be classified into three categories: the natural or physical, the supernatural, and the mystical. The natural or physical means the mere dysfunction of the physical body system or mere injury caused by accident. This type of diseases will normally respond to medicine quickly. Supernatural and mystical diseases are the ones caused by witches and wizards by breaking taboos, neglecting one's responsibilities to ancestors, and disharmony with fellow human being. Sometimes these are usually difficult to treat except with special combination of treatment of herbs and ritual, confession, sacrifices and special restoration of disharmony against God and divinities, spirits, and the entire environment. Before the advent of Christianity and Western medicine, Africans have developed certain effective ways of rescuing themselves from these types of diseases. These ways include the use of herbs, powerful, mysterious or potent words, animal parts, living and non-living things, water, fasting, prayers, laying of hands, and other rituals for restoration of the harmony among the people and the environment.

Massaging, as a therapeutic system, is another important system of healing, which is effective for the treatment of nervous, muscular systems, and especially the treating of gynecological problems.[3] Hydrotherapy involves the use of cold, or hot water. Compress and steam vapor baths is used for different diseases like headache, fever rheumatism, and general pains. Hot water relaxes the skin capillaries and the activity of the sweat glands.[4] It has been established that water increases the consumption of oxygen up to about 75% and it eliminates about 85% of carbon dioxide in the body.[5] Fasting is an important aspect of indigenous therapeutic methods in Africa. To cure an ailment, patients are instructed to abstain from food for certain period of days or weeks. This method is usually used for curing obesity, indigestion, overweight, mental and some chronic diseases. Mume was very sure of the positive result of fasting in curing diseases when he says that fasting is the most effective means of body house cleaning known. Fasting is an eliminator of accumulated toxins as well as a general restorative. Fasting is a purifying process. It brings about a rapid elimination of toxic elements and poisonous materials from the body.[6]

Another important method of healing is what we may call faith-healing method. In African Indigenous Religion, especially in ancestor worship, a person who is tortured by the ancestors is asked to confess and make sacrifices. After all these have been done, the offender is made to believe that he has been forgiven and healed of the sickness.

The use of potent words, for therapeutic purposes is not uncommon among African indigenous people. These words have to be uttered in a specific place, at specific time and in a specific way for them to be effective. It may also involve ritual performances. Below is an example of the use of potent words[7] for healing. After chewing seven alligator pepper, and placing one's mouth on the patient's navel one should recite the potent words below to cure scorpion sting or headache:

Oorun lode l'alamu wonu,
Oorun kuju alaamu jade (7 times)

Translation:

When the sun is rises the female lizard disappears
When the sun sets the female lizard appears (7 times).[8]

Another important potent words for pregnant women for the purpose of safe and easy delivery is:

Kankan l'ewe ina njomo
Kan kan ni ki lagbaja omo lagbaja
bi mo re loni
Konu koho ki roju ti fifi aso re toro
Ki laghaja omo laghaja a ma
roju ti ofi bi omo re loni

Translation

The leave of *ina* burns in haste
(name the labouring woman)
the daughter of (name her mother)
should deliver her child in haste today
The *Konu koho* tree does not hesitate
to give off its cloth back (name the labouring woman)
The daughter of (name the mother)
should not hesitate to deliver her child today
Because the snake sheds it skin easily without problem.[9]

Immediately a woman who has a history of miscarriages or infant mortality is aware that she is pregnant, she should start using concoction meant for pregnant women called, *Agbo aboyun*. Two people closely related to me affirmed the efficacy of such medicine. Mr. Ayodele Michael[10] confirmed his use of concoction for his wife during pregnancy. This concoction was made of roots and leaves of trees boiled for drinking and bathing by his pregnant wife. My in-law, Mr. Balogun Aiyelehin narrated another story of when he went to visit his son in the northern part of Nigeria. According to him, his son complained about a regular painful birth despite the wife's regular visit to the orthodox hospitals. The native doctor prescribed a concoction for her for bathing and drinking. The result was an easy childbirth.[11]

In African culture, marriage and child bearing are considered to be the main focus of life. The inability to procreate is also considered a catastrophe that leads to polygamy and marriage failure, ridicule, and general unhappiness. The Yoruba people of Nigeria sought the knowledge of the cause of such bareness in women and the medicine to cure such diseases. The most serious of these diseases is called *eda* (leucorrhoea). This is serious because they recognize the fact that it does not respond quickly to treatment.[12] Among the medicines used to cure *eda* before the advent of the missionaries were:

> A fresh (*segirri or tagi iri*) adenopus brevifloris, spring onions, sulphur and local pap (*eko*). After the coat of the adenoids revifloris has been scrapped off and cut into pieces, it will be mixed and burnt together with the spring onions in a broken pot. After the sulphur powder has been mixed with the ingredients above, the husband and wife will drink the pap (*eko*) with it three times a day. They must have intercourse in the very day of use, but must wait for three days before another intercourse. Grind together ten bitter-cola, ten alligator pepper, ten kola-nuts, one snail, potash (*konwun*), onion salt, part of the feather of night jar bird (*emo ajao*), and drink the powder with maize pap (*eko agbado*) every morning.[13]

The Yorubas through their experiences identified another disease that is associated with catatonia discharge of women. Women who missed their menstruation for several months without any pregnancy (amenorrhea) are advised to use an indigenous medicine called *alase obinrin* which will eventually open up her menses and consequently bring about pregnancy. Such disease can be treated as follows:

> Potash (*konwun*), leaves of the herb *uraria picta papilonacae* (*alupayida*), the stalk of white guinea-corn (*poroporo baba funfun*), red parrot feathers (*ikoode*), stalk of white guinea corn potash, cam wood (*osun*), one bottle of

> coco-nut water, one bottle of palm kernel oil, one bottle of lime juice. A very hot fire-heated stone must be put in the medicine while still very hot and drink in the morning.[14]

The Yorubas of Nigeria have numerous medicines to accelerate the discharge of placenta (*oni bi or amubi*) to accelerate an easy birth for a woman in difficult labor. One of the prescriptions is as follows:

> a snake that has swallowed something. Remove and burn what has been swallowed with alligator pepper. The powder must be put in small gourd (*ado*) and cover with a white leather. The snake itself must be burnt separately with alligator pepper and a cowry, put in another small gourd and covered with red leather. When a woman is in a labor stage, she must be given (with a left hand and received with a left hand),[15]the powder in the small gourd with a red leather to drink with maize pap (eko). After few minutes with the same method the powder in the small gourd covered with white leather. The baby and the placenta will come
> immediately.[16]

There are some indigenous medicine readily available for some common sicknesses such as migraine headache, malaria, piles, cough, and others. For migraine headaches, Urhobo people of Delta State, Nigeria prepares *Adjuge* roots, taken from the ground without washing, then gently taking it with hand, it should be scraped on a leaf or leaves. Alligator pepper and some water should be added. The concoction must be dropped into patient's eyes like an eye drop.[17] Another important medicine for migraine headache is *materia medica* which must be applied between 4.P.M and 5 P.M when the sun is setting and when the patient faces the sun. The *materia medica* must be rubbed on the exact spot where the patient feels the pain. This rubbing must be repeated continuously until the patient feels no more pain after shaking his or her head.[18]

An effective medicine for stomach ache include chewing allegator pepper (9 for male and 7 for female) in the mouth and while the mouth is still hot, the following words should be recited:

Okun t'o wo nu o jade

Okun t'o wo igbo ni anpe ni ejo igbo
Okun t'o wo ile ni anpe ni ekolo
Okun t'o wo inu ni anpe ni ejo inu
Aringindin ni oruko ti anpe
Iwo edo---inu ma se run (mention the name of the patient) mo.

Translation

Okun that enters the stomach does not come out
Okun that enters the forest is what we call snake forest
Okun that enters the house is what we call *ekolo*
Okun that enters the stomach is what we call stomach
snake
We call it *Aringindin*
Iwo edo- stomach pain do not pain (mention the name of
the patient)
Spit the chewed allegator pepper on the belly of the patient and the
patient is released.[19]

Apart from the testimony concerning the efficacy of African indigenous medicine (as a result of my personal experience) mentioned above, there are other evidences and written testimonies. Rev. Fr. Julian Gorju affirmed the fact that even though the indigenous healers may not have the idea of accurate dosages of their medicine, their remedies are astonishingly efficacious.[20]

Mr. Akinwumi confirms the efficacy of the indigenous medicine:

The main objective of any art of healing is the ultimate achievement of a lasting cure. In fact, there have been cases where orthodox medicine failed and the traditional medicine proved useful in the treatment of chronic diseases.[21]

M. Gelfand mentioned a medicine woman who treats asthma effectively with a stramonium leaf despite the fact that she lives in a very remote village.[22] Mr. E.A Ohiaeri reported the effective treatment of snakebite with indigenous medicine at the University of Nigerian Nsukka, at the Traditional Nigerian Medical Centre. According to him six victims snakebite of the dangerous carpet viper (Nsukka's most dangerous snake) were treated successfully without any occurrence of relapse. The relief from the pain took approximately seven minutes after the administration of the indigenous remedies.[23] Prof. Lambo, Dr. Folayele Awosika, specialist in Clinical Pharmacy and Herbal Medicine, Abimbola Sodipe, President of the Nigerian Union of Medical Herbal Practitioners, Prof Ade Dopamu and others strongly affirm the efficacy of the indigenous medicine.[24]

Reading and Interpreting the Bible Therapeutically

As stated above, with the advent of Christianity in Africa, the indigenous therapeutic method was considered not only barbaric and fetish, but an abomination to Christianity. With total devotion of missionaries who left their beautiful countries to the so called African jungle, and with the emphasis on the importance of the Christian book, African Christian believe that there must be something equally potent in the Bible which could be used for healing. The discovery of passages that narrate stories of miraculous healing by words, actions, and herbs aroused great interest in the book of the Bible for healing. They therefore believed that the missionaries did not want to reveal that potent power in the Bible to them. They searched the Bible to find that power which the missionaries did not want to show them. According to them, they found that power and potent words in the Bible especially in the book of Psalms. Some Psalms are therefore, classified as therapeutic Psalms. The reading of the Bible is combined with African indigenous method of healing. Absolute faith in the word of God and in God himself is maintained but with the combination of herbs, prayer, fasting, and the use of the name of God in the healing process. It is believed that virtually all types of illnesses are curable with the combination of reading the Bible and the use of African materials.

Stomach Trouble

According to T.N.Adeboyejo,[25] Psalm 1, 2, and 3 are special Psalms for stomach pain. According to him, for these Psalms to be effective one should read them into water and pronounce the holy name of God, *Walola Asabata Jah* forty eight times. Mix together fried oil, potash, salt and fresh egg and sip it little by little. There is a perfect assurance that the stomach pain will disappear.

For swollen stomach, he recommends Pslams 20 and 40. One should get water from a flowing river into a new clay pot. Put together a complete palm front and three new mature palm leaf in the clay pot. While reading Pslam 20 and 40 with the holy name *Eli Sabatani* sixty two times. The reader must light nine candles and bathe with the water for nine days. Or these Psalms could be read into mixed fried oil, coconut oil, cow urine and shear butter oil. The Holy name above could also be read over it for drinking, bathing and rubbing over the body.

To clean dirts from a woman's stomach one should get a little kerosine, with shear butter, grand nut oil, and white alum, mix them. Read Psalm 50 six times into it, with the holy name *Eli-Ala*, God for 26 times. Offer a purification prayer and light three candles.[26] In order to cure stone in a woman's stomach, one should fill a new pot with water, put a small strong iron in it, light three candles and read Psalms 24 seven times with the holy name *Alola Lajaka Karara* 7 times. Do this for seven days and bath the water for seven days. One can also make oil for the healing. In this case mix ground nut oil, one egg, white and black alum and read Psalm 28 and purify it with the holy names *Jah Eli Ala* 21 times for drinking.[27]

For stomach trouble of any kind Adeboyejo[28] also recommends a mixture of a half bottle of dry gin, one bottle of *bintu* (perfume) a bottle of olive oil, three *Kanfo*, one *Kafura*, few alum. Tie the bottle with a palm front at the neck. Pray and fast for three days without food or water (white fasting) to purify the bottle and the content. Read Psalms 19, 24, 53, 54, 115 thrice, read Isaiah 47 seven times, Hebrew 11, Luke 9:2-7; 10:9-16 for three days with the following holy names *Bilasulika, Labilasu, Hubasabilahhuka* seven times, *Jehovah Araji* three times, *Salajah Eloi* three times. *Yod He Vau He* seven times and *Wasara* seven times. Pray for victory in different kinds of ways over it. Drink two full spoon every morning and night.

Bareness

One of the major problems in Africa is bareness and infant mortality. These are mostly responsible for family break up and polygamy. In most indigenous societies in Africa, as priests and diviners are contacted before any marriage contract to make sure that the spouse will not be barren or experience infant mortality, so also have some therapeutic Psalmsand the Bible passages have been identified as effective cure for such problems. For barren women to have children, Psalms 51, Gen. 15.1-5, 21.1-8, I Sam. 1.9-20 should be read three times into coconut water or raw native egg with prayer and drink the water. The action above should take place very early in the morning while naked and after a woman might have had sexual intercourse with her husband. The following names should be pronounced for effectiveness: *Jehovah Shiklo-hirami* 21 times *and Holy Mary* 12 times.[29] So also if a woman is barren, get ocean water, 7 limes, honey, and original perfume. Take them to the mercy land for three days. Start from midnight on Tuesday. Be happy always. Face your husband alone and eat much fruits, banana, oranges and coconut. Put on heavy incense in your house every night and sprinkle perfume. Put three crosses in the water. Sing three songs for forgiveness of sins with your husband. Sing three songs for mercy and three for praises. Call the following holy names: Jehovah, Jesus Christ, Holy Michael, *El Shadai, Jehova-Jireh, El-braka-bred-El* 21 times. Read also Genesis 21:1-8 twenty-one times every night. A wife and husband should pray naked while facing the four corners of the house, starting from the east. Thank God that He has done it and roll to the right and left. In your prayer remind God of His promises in Genesis for human being to multiply. Remind Him of his promises to Sarah, Elizabeth and Hannah and all were fulfilled. Give thanks to God confidently that He has done it. Give thanks with three types of fruits to God every Wednesday or Sunday with honey, sugar and salt. If you cannot find mercy land water, use direct rain from above which has not touched any place except your container. Get used to sleeping in the mercy land on Tuesday nights with three candles before the Lord. Pray always around the mercy land on Wednesday and Sundays. Repeat this every month.[30] For barrenness he[31] also recommends the reading of Psalms 3, 8, and 12 every morning. Every evening read Psalm 4, 8 and 121. Always pray and remind God that if you were not born by your mother you would not exist. Tell God that it is His wish and commandment to multiply. Ask God to bless your womb so that the unbelievers would praise His name as soon as possible. Make a promise that you would praise Him as long as you live if He blesses your womb.

According to Ogunfuye,[32] Psalm 1 that compares the way of the wicked with the righteous is used therapeutically to cure gyneacological problems such as miscarriages in women. Immediately a woman is aware that she is pregnant, she should read Psalm 1 daily in the morning and evening. The process should be accompanied by prayer in the name of *Eli-Ishaddi, Jehovah shallom.*

Safe delivery

For safe delivery, Adewole recommends the reading of Psalms 34, 59, 60 into a rock water. Drink and bathe it on Monday, Wednesday, and Friday. Call Holy Mother Mary.[33]

Ogunfuye[34] recommends Psalms 126 which is also a prayer to God to restore Israelite fortunes. This is efficacious for infant mortality. A woman with a history of past experiences of infant mortality should start reading this Psalm immediately she is aware of her pregnancy. This Psalm should be read into water for bathing, washing, and drinking daily throughout the period of her pregnancy. The same process should also continue immediately after delivery to wash the baby until it is fully grown. With the reading of this Psalms as instructed, early death of such child is unthinkable. Psalm 126 could also be written on four pure parchments with the holy names *Sinni, Sinsuni and Semanflaf.* Keep it in the four corners of a house whenever a person with the history of born-to-die children (*abiku* in Yoruba and *ogbanje* in Ibo of Nigeria) is pregnant. Psalm 16 is recommended for safe and easy safe delivery. It is to be read three times over water by a pregnant woman for drinking and bathing with holy name *JEHOVAH JARRABBILLAH* three times.

For general healing Adeboyejo[35] recommends several passages. Psalm 18 can be read over a sick person with the holy name *Eli- Laja* once. This should be done with fervent prayer for healing. For physical pain Psalms 21 should be read over water from a well eight times and pour one raw egg into the water for bathing with the pronunciation of the names *Eli Eli Laha Baha* ten times. This could be done as many times as possible.

Defective Hearing

For defective hearing take banana water from its rotten tree. Mix this with little petro, egg, and few gun powder and read Psalm 16 to it three times with the holy name *Eliala* pronounced 50 times.

Drop the water in the ear after anointing the ear. Or read Psalm 119:169-176 over onion juice for three days. Get few drops into the ear and one would be healed. [36]

Cough

For cough take honey, palm oil, mix them together, read Psalm 24, 84, 91 three times. Each time call the holy names *Jah-Kurajah Jah Kulah* three times at every reading of the Psalm. The mixture should be taken regularly. Pray and wait for the power of God.[37] For cough, Psalm 7 can be read over water once for drinking and bathing with the name *Elilaja* 7 times.[38]

Babies Sicknessess

For illness that affect baby's head (*Oka*) some water, olive oil, little potash and some blue alum. Read Psalms 2 over the water with the pronunciation of the holy name *Huratala-Lakaja* ten times use the water to bath and use the oil to rub the place.[39]

Prayer for born to die children. Pour water in a pot, light 7 candles and put them on your palm and dip the candles in the water to quench the light. Call the holy names into the water *Eli-Lah, Elilah, Elilah, Alolah, Alolah Elola, Lah Eloi Alah Eloi Alah* 62 times. The water should be used to bathe at a road junction. One should also mix coconut water, ground nut oil or mellon oil, few potash, and blue alum with the holy names above for drinking and for robbing on the body.[40]

For a baby who does not walk on time, fill an earthen pot with water, put ten leaves of palm front in it and read Proverbs 9 while lighting ten candles round the pot. Call the holy names *Alala Ho Ho Ho Ha Ha Ha Eli* Samuel 100 times. Pray "mindfully" for bathing and drinking and then remove the palm leaves after the prayer.[41]

Small Pox

Prophet Adewole[42] recommends Psalm 84 to be read ten times over water with the holy name *Alojah Alojah Alojah* to be pronounced 21 time. Or a mixture of fried oil, potash, shear butter, with the reading of Psalm 84 to it. The oil is for rubbing the body and the water for bathing.

Epilepsy

For Epilepsy, mix beach ocean lagoon, and tap water together. Read Psalm 109, 102, 100 once to it with the holy name *Elilahajah* 80 times for drinking and bathing. One can also mix oil with fresh grinded scaly fish, shear butter, the bile of a cow (*ororo malu*), an egg. Read the above Psalm and the holy names for rubbing and licking.[43]

Chronic Illnesses and other ailments

Treatment for Chronic illness, fill a new pot with water and read Psalms 21 twenty times and light 12 candles round the pot. Call the holy names *Dabola Elilajah* and use the water for bathing and drinking. One can also mix coconut oil, shear butter, one egg and read Psalms 21 and the holy names above for drinking and rubbing on the body. Offer prayer for purification.[44]

For convulsion read Psalm 1 over water for drinking and bathing and pronounce the holy name *Hela Hola* 84 times on the head of the sick person. Or mix oil, dry gin or brandy with potash, blue alum, and read Psalm 1 with the holy name above for drinking and robbing on the body.[45] Bolarinwa[46] also believes that these Psalms are potent for curing toothache, headache and backache. For toothache, these psalms must be read into a luke warm water and the patient rinses his mouth with it until the tumbler is empty. The process can be repeated from time to time.

For boil, pour water in a pot with three pebbles and read Psalm 3 to it with a fresh egg and olive oil. One should rub the spot with the mixture and bath with the water.[47]

In order to cure menopause, a woman should pour water in a big white pan or bucket full of water and read Psalm 94 to it thrice and purify the water with the holy name *Ajawolah-Takubbah* seven times. This should be done for three days and each time this is done there should be prayer offered each time. Divide the water into two, one part for drinking, and the other part for dipping her waist in it every morning before talking to any person.[48]

Someone with a serious headache should read Psalms 3, 24, Genesis 1:1-31 seven times with the holy names *Jehovah-Adonai* seven times. One should pray for victory and healing of that headche into the water and wash the head into a deep hole. The hole should be covered after washing the head.[49]

For healing different sicknesses Adeboyejo[50] says:
Do not talk to anybody in the morning when you are going to get ocean water and lagoon. Sing the song of spirit of the devil move. Salutation to Thee King of Cherub or song of Great Physician is here and then read Psalms 51 thrice, 25 and 24 once. Pray for forgiveness of sin for the person. Call these holy names *Jah-Elli-Rabnaittah* seven times. However, for all kinds of sickness, Adewole recommends the reading of Psalm 62:1-12 thrice, Mark 5:1-43 once, Mark 7: 24-37, Mark 16:14-24 over the water for drinking and bathing.[51] Ogunfuye recommended Psalm 41 for general healing of all kinds of diseases.[52] According to him when this Psalm is read repeatedly everyday, God would come in defence of the reader and the prayer would be answered. Psalm 49 is to overcome serious illness. This Psalm should be written with a new pen and a new ink with the name of God *Schaddei* on pure parchment (sheep parchment).

Chief Oguntuye recognises Psalm 6 as the one to relieve a sick person of pains and worries. According to him it is also good for stomach trouble, eye trouble or any ailment. The sick person should read the Psalm in great humility and with special prayer and the mentioning of the holy names *Jaschaja; Bali; Hashina* in mind. According to him all her worries will be removed. Below is the special prayer to be offered to accompany this Psalm for effective healing:

> O Lord God and Prince of Peace, I beseech Thee in the name of *Jaschaja, Bali, Hashina* to hear me and speedily heal me from these diseases that troubles me (name the diseases). Wipe away my tears and turn my sorrow into joy. Give unto me Thy wonderful grace to overcome all manner of diseases. Restore unto me my former health and silent all my adversaries for ever. Forgive me all my sins and sustain me with Thy grace all the days of my life. Pour thy blessings upon me from above and let my prayers be acceptable in Thy sight so that I may glorify thy holy name forever. Amen.[53]

If the patient does not know how to read, someone should read for him or her but someone must mention the mother's name.

Endnotes

[1] This is not an attempt to blame the Christian missionaries for African woes. Despite all the mistakes that Christian missionaries have made, it is an indisputable fact that they have been immense blessing to Africa is in the area of education. They did not only translated the Bible into African languages, they have also taught Africans how to read the Bible in their languages and "with their own eyes." This enables African Christians to read the Bible with their own cultural perspectives. Justin Ukpong, " Reading the Bible with African Eyes," *Journal of Theology for Southern Africa (JTSA)*, (June 1995),3-14.

[2] D.C. Silis, *International Encyclopaedia of Social Science*, vol 5 and 6 (New York: Macmillan Press, 1972), 95.

[3] J. Ubrurhe, " Life and Healing Processes in Urhobo Medicine," *Humanitas* (1994) vol. 1, New Series, forth coming.

[4] Ibid.

Endnotes

[5] Ibid.

[6] J.O Mume, *Traditional Medicine in Nigeria* (Agbarho: Jom Tradomedical naturopathic Hospital ,1978), 65. Eight therapeudic methods in Urhobo medicine are mentioned by Mume.

[7] As said earlier, the term "potent words" is preferable to the so-called incantation which the Eurocentric missionaries, anthropologies, sociologies derogatorily forced on an aspect of African health system, simply because they do not understand how it works.

[8] Ademiluka, "The Use of Psalms in African Context," 80

[9] *Secrets,* 72-73.

[10] Mr. Ayodele is a lecturer in the Department of Botany, Delta State University, Abraka, Nigeria.

[11] Mr. Balogun Aiyelehin lives at Bagido , Isanlu, Kogi State, Nigeria. When I asked him of the type of concortion he refused to tell me for the fear hat I might do it without patronizing him.

[12] Dopamu, "Obsterics and Gynaecology Amongl the Yoruba," *Orita* ,vol. XIV/1 (June 1982), 34-42

[13] Ibid.

[14] Ibid. 37

[15] Ibid.

[16] Ibid

[17] J.O Ubrurhe," Urhobo Traditional Medicine, " A PhD dissertation, University of Nigeria,

Endnotes

Nsukka, 1994, 49

[18]ibid.

[19] This prescription is from Mr. Tola Agoro, who was the Assitant Chaplain at Interdenominational Chapel, Delta State University, Abraka, Delta State, Nigeria.

[20]Ethnography of the English Part of the Vicoriat of Uganda," and "Busawo of Buganda:The Traditional Doctors of Buganda," in *African Therapeutic System*, 141

[21]" Research in Native Medicne," Daily Times, Sept 25, (1975), 8.

[22]*Medicine and Custom in Africa (Edinburgh and London: E&S Livingstone, 1964),4.*

[23]*Report of a Research in Nige rian Traditional Medicine, medical Centre*, University of Nigeria, Nigeria, nd, 6.

[24]See Dopamu, "The Place of Onisegun....," 220ff. Sunday Sketfch, Feb. 2, (1986), and "Traditional Medicine Revisited," in *Daily Times*, Aug. 12, (1975),7.

[25] Prophet Sam Akin Adewole, *The Revelation of God for 1992 and the Years Ahead* (Lagos: Sam Adewole, 1991), 21

[26] Ibid., 20

[27] Ibid., 21

[28] Ibid, 42

[29] Prophet Samuel Akin Adewole, *The Revelations of God for 1992 and the Years Ahead Plus some Effective special Psalms to solve various Problems* (Lagos: Celetial Church of Christ, 1991), 22

Endnotes

[30] Ibid., 44-45

[31] Ibid., 21

[32] J.O Ogunfuye, *The Secrets of the Uses of Psalms*, Third Edition (Ibadan: Ogunfuye Publication, no date), 78 ?

[33] Adewole, 25

[34] Ogunfuye, 78 ?

[35] Adeboyejo, 16

[36] Ibid.

[37] Adewole, 42

[38] Ibid

[39] ibid., 20

[40] Ibid .

[41] Ibid., 21

[42] Ibid. 22

[43] Ibid.,

[44] Ibid., 23

[45] Ibid.

Endnotes

[46] J.A. Bolarinwa, *Potency and Efficacy of Psalms* (Ibadan: Oluseyi Press, no date), 67

[47] Adewole, 26

[48] Ibid., 28

[49] Ibid.

[50] Adeboyejo, 16 ?

[51] Adewole, 36

[52] Ogunfuye, ?

[53] J.O Ogunfuye, *The Secrets of the Uses of Psalms*, Third Edition (Ibadan: Ogunfuye Publication, no date), 78.

CHAPTER VI

Reading and Interpreting the Bible for Protection in Life

Protection in African Religious Tradition

All over the world people are concerned with protection. Protection against destruction of crops, clothes, houses, land, trees, water, and other things that cannot be named are essential in human life. Protection against destruction of human being is most seriously sought.

The nature and process of protection by African indigenous people is remarkably different from the Western world. This is because Africans living in the continent face some peculiar problems due to their perception of world around them. To indigenous Africans the presence of evil, witches, sorcerers, evil spirits, and all different kinds of enemies are painfully real. They believe that they are responsible for all the evil things that happen all over the world. In Africa indigenous tradition, all means are used to protect children, young, and adult. These include the use of animate and inanimate things, such as stones, sand, trees, leaves, human parts, animals, water, urine, and whatever can be mentioned. This reflects the seriousness of protection in African indigenous tradition.

Among the Yoruba people of Nigeria, there is a belief that every person has at least one known or unknown enemy called *ota*. There are two types of enemies among the Yorubas of Nigeria. The first type is brought by some perennial quarrels, which come from variety of circumstances such as land disputes, property inheritance, chieftancy titles disputes and constant rivalries among wives in polygamous homes. The second type is called *Aye* (literally means the world). These are sorcerers, witches and all persons who are inherently wicked and malicious by nature. They are more dreadful than the first group of enemies. They go to the extent of employing professional medicine person to harm their enemies. Various techniques are used in harming the enemies. Potent powerful words (so-called incantations) pronounced on charms such as *epe*, (curse), *isaasi, apeta, ironsi* and *eedi* are used.[1] The result of such charms can be painful. It may be abnormal behavior, sudden loss of children and property, chronic illness and even death. To express how powerful and wicked is the activities of witches, Primate J.O.S Ayelabola states the confession of a witch:

> We drink human blood in the day or night;
> We can prevent a sore from healing;
> We can make a person to lose a large sum of money;
> We can reduce a great man to nothing;
> We can send a small child to heaven suddenly;
> We can cause a woman to bear born-to-die children (*abiku*).[2]

Before the advent of Christianity, Africans have a cultural way of dealing with the problem of enemies and all evildoers. There are various techniques of making use of natural materials and potent powerful words, which they put to defensive and offensive use in dealing with evil ones. One of these cultural ways of protection against enemies is the use of imprecatory potent words (the so-called incantations) called *ogede* in Yoruba language. Traditionally when an African identifies an enemy and he or she himself or herself does not have the potent words or medicine to deal with such enemy, such a person consults a medicine man (*babalawo* or *onisegun* or *oologun* in Yoruba language) who prepares or teaches him or her some potent words or give a charm for protection or for attacking the enemy. The words must be recited at certain place, at certain time of the day or night, and for certain number of times for such words to be effective. Usually, people who want protection at the time of traveling or hunting, for protection at home go to a particular priest called *babalawo* or *onisegun* or *oologun* (in Yoruba language), who are gifted and well disciplined in the art.

There are three major ways of protection in African indigenous tradition. They are through the use of potent words, called *ogede*, the use of medicine called *tira*, and other medicine for the body. A perfect example of the type of potent words used among the Yoruba society at the approach of an enemy.

O di oluworo-ji-woro	it becomes oluworo ji-woro
Odi oluworo-ji-woro	It becomes oluworo ji-woro
Oku aja kiigbo,	The dead dog does not bark
Oku agbo kiikan	the dead ram does not fight
Ewe gbigbe t' osubu lu odo	
o di gbere	The dried leaf that falls into the river is lost forever
Od'olu woro-ji-woro	It becomes oluworo ji-woro
Ki awon ota mi lo gbere	So let my enemies be lost forever
Oku aja niwon	They are dead dogs
Oku agbo niwon	They are dead rams
Ewe gbigbe niwon.	They are dried leaves.[3]

More examples of potent words for protection against witches and wizard in the African indigenous tradition are numerous. However, it suffice to mention one more:

> *Igbagbe se oro ko lewe (3 times)*
> *Igbagbe se afomo ko legbo (3*
> *Igbagbe se Olodumare ko ranti la*
> *ese pepeye*
> *Nijo ti pepeye ba daran egba igbe*
> *hoho ni imu bo 'nu*
> *Ki igbagbe se lagbaja omo lagbaja*
> *ko maa wogbo lo*
> *Tori t'odo ba nsan ki iwo ehin moo......*

Translation

> Due to forgetfulness the
> oro(cactus) *plant has no*
> *leaves (3 times)*
> Due to forgetfullness the *afomo (misleoes)*
> plant has no roots (3 times)

69

> Due to forgetfullness god did not remember to
> separate the toes of the dock (3times)
> When the duck is beaten it cries, *hoho*
> May forrgetfullness come upon
> (name the enemy) the daughter of
> name the mother); that is, may he
> loose his senses That he or she may
> enter into bush Because a flowing river
> does not flow backward (and so on).[4]

These words when recited many times, would make the witches and enemies trying to attack get lost in the bush or in the cities. It will make them forget all the evil actions planned against a person reciting the potent words. As already discussed above in the section of African worldview, words are power and can be used for good or for evil.

Another major way of obtaining protection against enemies in African societies is the use of charms or amulets. Amulets and charms are usually obtained from medicine men that are healers and diviners. They are called *tira* in Yoruba language of Nigeria. They are used for diverse purposes but mainly as protective devices to prevent enemies, witches and wizard, and evil spirits from entering a house and attacking a person. It is also used to nullify all the attempts of enemies or sorcerers. They are prepared with different ingredients according to the purpose of the charm or amulets. For example, a charm for the purpose of hanging on the doorframe for protection may be made of "seven leaves of some plants, and seven seed of alligator pepper." Charms to be tied around one's neck for protection against enemies may require alligator peppers, white and red cola-nuts and the blood of a cock. Charms are wrapped with animal skin and sewn round. Others are wrapped inside pieces of cloth or paper and tied with some black and white threads. Some also require the recitation of some potent words and prayer to go along with the charms for their effectiveness.[5]   Those words must be recited exactly according to the prescription of the medicine man otherwise it may not be efficacious.

In traditional Africa, hunters who hunt in the bush at night would normally protect themselves with charms against wild animal attack, snakebites, and against wicked supernatural beings such as *iwin* and *aanjonu* (spirits). The *tira* against accident or crash is called *egbe* in Yoruba language. An example of a protective charm can be prepared with the dried head of poor father snake (*oka*), chameleon, alligator pepper, all dried and grinded into powder and wrapped with the skin of a tiger and used as belt. The following words are to be said: "Poor father snake has no animal to fear, chameleon has no insect to fear and tiger has no animal to fear. So the user will not fear any foe."[6]

Other medicines for protection are numerous. There are cutlass proof and bulletproof medicines. An example of cutlass proof medicine has the ingredients of seven black pepper leaves, seven seeds of alligator pepper and one native egg. The leaves and the boiled egg must be chewed alone. One must avoid eating any raw palm oil and avoid day light sexual intercourse.

Medicine for protection against witchcraft has the ingredient of seven young leaves of *iroko* (mahogany) tree, one seed of alligator pepper, a bucket of water, and a stick with fire. All these items should be put in bucket of water. After the leaves have been squeezed, put the stick with fire inside the water. Throw the stick with fire forward until the parts with fire points outside. Use the concoction to bathe while saying these words. " Nobody can hold python because of its awe. Even if water is insipid it quenches fire."[7]

Other medicines include:
(1) *Sokuro*- Medicine hung up to prevent death
(2) *Arimole*- Medicine buried in the ground for self protection
(3) *Ogadagodo*- Padlocks used for law suits so that judges will not remember certain cases or judge amiss

(5)   *Sinsin gbere*- Skin marks with blades with powdered medicine
for protection against witches, or snakebites or good luck-success
in schoolwork.
Modarikan-Medicineforprotectionagainstenemy's
medicine to turn back evil medicine against those sending it.

Reading and Interpreting the Bible for Protection

When Christian missionaries arrived in Africa, the converts were
forbidden to use African indigenous medicine, that is, potent
words, talisman, and even herbal medicine for protection. They
were told that it was abominable to Christianity. The missionaries,
with good intention to promote the kingdom of Christ, did not
only build schools, but they built maternities, dispensaries, and
hospitals where orthodox medicine was dispensed. The truth,
however, is that the hospitals, dispensaries and maternity were not
enough for the people. Those who were fortunate enough to have
access to these hospitals and maternities, could not afford to pay
for the cost of orthodox medicine. The result was that not all
Nigerians had access to the orthodox medicine. Others who have
access to this orthodox medicine and were able to pay for them
still had problems of dealing with what they believed to be the
source of the diseases, and misfortune, and they sought protection
from what befell them. Hospitals could not deal effectively with
that aspect of African belief.

When they accepted Christianity and threw away their
potent words, charms, and all kind of medicine, they did that with
the belief that there would be a better substitute for them for
protection, healing, and success. The unfortunate thing however, is
that the missionaries did not teach them the source of the white
man's power which they thought must be present in the so called,
White man's religion. They were disappointed, and therefore, they
took law into their own hands by using the Christian book and the

traditional means for protection, healing and success. Many were excommunicated from the mainline churches. When others who remained in the missionary churches searched in vain for that substitute in the missionary Christianity they accepted. They believed that the missionaries were hiding that power from them, and that they would never discover that power unless they break away.[8] The inevitable result was the breaking away from the missionary churches. Determined to find that greater power in Christianity, they search the Bible in their own way.

Edward Blyden, a Dutch West Indies born Presbyterian, who rejected some of the claims of the anthropologists that white people were superior to black people, influenced the establishment of indigenous African churches. He further maintained that the evangelization of Africa would never be successful until it was taken from the hand of he White man who imposed alien forms of evangelization on Africans. The first noticeable indigenous church formed was the United Native African Church in Lagos, Nigeria in 1891. As a result of dissatisfaction with the dictatorial missionaries, foreign formalism which sometimes led to the quenching of the spirit, and against the foreign anti-African customs, laws, dancing, family, marriage, and etiquette, the African Church Organization was formed in 1901 and many prophetic figures emerged.

The separation gave them the freedom to search the Bible to discover that which supposedly was hidden power. The book of Psalms was the most favorite book read that contained that power for protection, healing, and success. As discussed above, the most serious concern among Africans is power for protection as a result of their strong and realistic belief in the existence of enemies who are to be attributed to witches, wizards, and evil spirits that fill African forest. They approach the Bible and use it with the same method that the indigenous African people used to deal with the problem of enemies and seek protection against enemies. They used the entire Bible as potent words, charms, and medicine to combat evil forces and to protect them against such forces of evil.

The methods of using the Bible for protection in African Indigenous Churches can be classified into three major ways. Below are the three ways of using the Bible as charms, potent words and medicine for protection.

The Bible as Potent Words for Protection

Mr. T. N. Adeboyejo was emphatic concerning the use of Bible as "incantation and shield for Christians." He says,

> I implore everybody to endeavor to read Holy Bible after this special arrangement especially every time because BIBLE is the word of Son of Mary, particularly it was incantation and shield for Christians. I beg you in the name of Merciful God to refrain from retaliation for yourself, because enemies will be foot for the children of God to reach the position of honor and glory.[9]

According to him, the following passages are to be used for protection for one day. Psalms 13, 46, 91, 116, 121, 125, and Job 5:18-27. These passages are wonderful words that can protect Christians for twenty-four hours. While reading these passages, one is instructed to pronounce the following holy names: *Esiel, Angla, Jehovah Emmanuel.* One must also say the following words: "See and know that I am He no God after me, I am He that can kill you and make you alive. I am He that can heal; nobody can escape from my power or shadow. I spread my hand toward the heaven. I said I am He who is living forever *ANIMO ANIMON, ALIMON, TAFTIAN.* The Lord saves and keeps me (Amen)." After pronouncing these holy names, some special prayers must be said,

> ...happiness belongs to the children of God, who are like the God Jehovah. Thou are my power and shield, sword in presence of my enemies, my enemies will run back. They   shall fall because God will be in His holy place, Everlasting God, command Thy angels who stationed at four corners of world Holy Michael, Gabriel, Raphael and Uriel to protect me and to fight my cause in all ways from today (Amen).[10]

All the above should be read three times before going anywhere so that these angels will protect one for twenty four hours and prevent any sudden death or harm.

For nearby enemies Psalm 1, 2, 5 and 10 are appropriate. If one has enemies running after someone and declaring war,

Psalm 10 must be recited. One should fast till twelve noon and pray three times, that is, in the morning, afternoon, and evening. The holy name *JARA TA AJAJA MOMIN* should be pronounce seven times.[11]

If one is planning to travel, recitation of Psalm 102:4-18 will protect one from any motor accident, ship wreck, air crash, and others. Evangelist Luke Jolugba who is the founder and pastor of Cherubim and Seraphim Church, Isanlu, Kogi State, Nigeria, considers reciting of Psalm 54 as the potent words to protect travelers.[12] However, Chief J.O Ogunfuye considers the reading of Psalms 17, 119:105-112 with some special prayers, as protection for travelers. According to him Psalm 17 should be recited when enemies are trying to make your journey a failure and you have no defense. This Psalm must be read with the holy name *Jerora* with the following prayers:

> O God my Savior, I beseech Thee in Thy power to come down from Thy heavenly abode and deliver me from all my adversaries who now compass round about me to do me evil. O Thou that heareth prayers, arise in Thy wrath and fight my cause. Scare them away and render them powerless against me. Save me from their wicked designs and prevent them from blocking my way of success in my proposed travels. Let Thy holy angels and guard me throughout my journey. Give me Thy holy sprit to overcome all obstacles. Give me grace and favour and let all my wishes been granted for the sake of Thy adorable holy name, *Jehovah Jerora*. Amen.[13]

Ogunfuye calls Psalm 119:105-112 *Nun* Psalm and the 14th division of the Psalm. It should be recited every morning and evening prayers, before embarking on any journey. If this is done, there is a guarantee that one will be safe and be successful in the journey.[14] An anonymous booklet, *The Uses of Psalms* considered Psalm 2, 64, 90, and 124 as protective Psalms while traveling on water, and dangerous roads.[15] T.N Adeboyejo also sees Psalm 102:4-18 as a protective Psalms when read with the name *OLITARAKAJAH* fourteen times before one leaves home for a journey. One will be delivered from motor, ship, canoe or wind accident.[16]

Chief Ogunfuye recognizes Psalm 60 as potent words for

soldiers, police and others going to war, and hunters going to hunt at night when read with appropriate prayer. The anonymous author of the booklet, *The Uses of Psalms* sees the same Psalm as potent words for protection for hunters and as bulletproof when used with the Holy name *JAH*.[17]

T.N Adeboyejo prescribes Psalm 14 and 36 as potent words for protection against someone trying to lie against a person. These Psalms should be read three times with the holy name *"MUPATEKA JEHOVAH AFENI"* and *"ELI SUMETE."*[18] Psalm 137 is included with 36 as potent words against slanderer with the following prayer:

> *EL-YAH, AGLA, ADONAI, JOD, HE, FOR, HE*: God of Abraham, God of Isaac and God of Jacob, God of Shadrach, Meshach and Abednego, God the Father, God the son and God the Holy Ghost, grant to us according to our hearts desires, Amen.[19]

Psalm 24 is considered potent words for protection against flood.[20] Psalm 116 is the word for protection against sudden death. According to Ogunfuye, Psalms 148 and 149 are considered potent words for the protection against fire.[21] While Psalm 147 is a protection against snakebite, 119:137-144 are considered potent words against dismissal from one's daily duty.[22] Psalms 51, 27, 9, 91, 109, Genesis 11:1-9, Matthew 15:29-38 are to be recited as potent words for protection against extravagance or wasteful spending.[23] Adeboyejo prescribes Psalm 84 to be read seven times with the holy name *BAPA BAPAJIH* ten times. Protection against oppression by rulers such as *obas*, chiefs, kings, emirs, governors and presidents requires the recitation of Psalm 51, II Chronicles 9:13-28; 17:1-13; 24:1-16; Psalm 93, 72 three times.[24] This should include the recitation of the holy name *Jah-Jehova, Jehova Emmanuel, Jehova Lass* seven times.

The Bible as Amulets or Charms for Protection

I have stated above that the use of charms or amulets is one of the indigenous ways for seeking protection in Africa. The African

Indigenous Churches make use of these methods in their approach to the interpretation of the Bible. Based on their belief in the power of words, the Bible is written on parchments, worn in the neck, hung on the doorpost of a house, or kept under a pillow overnight. Prayers are offered for the effectiveness of the charms.

The use of Bible as protection against enemies, witches, and wizard is a common phenomena in African Indigenous Churches in Nigeria. Prophet J.O Ogunfuye seems to specialize in the use of the Bible, especially the book of Psalms, for protection, cure and success. For protection against "secret enemies, evil doers and trouble mongers."[25] Psalm 7 should be written on a pure parchment and put in a special consecrated bag and kept under one's pillow. It should be written on the parchment with the special prayer below:

> O merciful Father, Almighty and everlasting King, I beseech Thee in the holy name of *Eel Elijon* to deliver me from all secret enemies and evil spirits that plan my destruction always. Protect me from their onslaught and let their evil forces be turned back upon them. Let their expectation come to naught and let them fail in their bid to injure me. Let their ways be dark and slippery and let thy holy angels disperse them so that they may not come nigh unto my dwelling place. Hear my prayer now for the sake of holy *Eel Elijon*. Amen.[26]

Ogunfuye also prescribes Psalm 126, 127 as a protection against evil spirit in children when written on the parchment. This is considered a very powerful Psalm to prevent born-to-die children from dying. The prescription is as follows:

Write this Psalm on four pure parchments with the holy names *Sinni*, *Sinsuni* and *Semanglaf* and then keep them in the four corners of your house. This should be done whenever your wife is pregnant and any child born unto you will live because he will be free from the molestation of evil spirits.[27]

Psalm 127 should be written in a pure parchment and then put in a special cloth bag to be tied on the neck of the child as soon as the child is born. By doing this the life of the child will be prolonged and will be free from the attacks of all those who hate him without cause.[28] Psalms 4, 9, 32, 70, 83, and other Psalms can be used as amulets to prevent all evils.[29] J. O Ogunfuye concludes his booklet on Psalms and their preparation.

> In this book you will read some Psalms, such as Psalms 4, 9, 32, and 70, 83, and Psalm 127, etc. are recommended to be written on the pure parchment as an object for protection and success. The other Psalms, which are not included in the Psalms as recommended above, will also be found very useful and to give the desired results if they are also written on pure parchments in the same way as the Psalms mentioned above. This should be done in addition to the constant reading of such Psalms which are recommended in this book, especially those Psalms for protection against evil spirits, evil occurrences, enemies, and for good luck, grace and favor, progress and for success in all undertakings.[30]

The Bible as Medicine for Protection

I have discussed above that one of the ways of mounting offensive and defensive battle against the evil ones and enemies in the African indigenous tradition is the use of herbal and non-herbal medicine. The reading and writing of the word of God in conjunction with herbal and non-herbal medicine, and the citing and reciting the holy names of God and angels to secure protection has become a way of life in African indigenous churches.

Psalms 51 should be read with the holy name *DAM-SELLAH JEHOVAH RAFFKKAH*, 32 with *JHOVAH OLLIFFIJJILLAH* and 130 with *JAH RAHAAM*.[31] While praying with the reading of these Psalms for three days (Sunday -Tuesday) with three candle sticks, one should confess and plead for forgiveness of his or her sins and that of one's generation. T.N Adeboyejo also prescribes Psalm 10, 14, 24, 28, 34, 50, 91, 110, 114, Isaiah 41:8-16, and 47 with special instruction. Below are his exact words:

> On Wednesday a white candle in each corner of your room three or two white candles, one yellow candle in the middle of the room, read these Ps. 10, 14, 110 and 114 each at the corner of the room in front of three candles at the middle, put bucket, pan or pot in which you have put palm front inside then. Put calabash of water near it, read Ps. 28, 91 and Isaiah 41:8-16 into the water in the bucket. Read Ps.17, 50 and Isaiah 47 into the water inside calabash. After all these read Ps. 24 for the seal of it. Pray for

redemption from all powers of Satan and all evil doers, in and outside of your body over the water in the bucket, then pray for victory over all your enemies. Ask God to let them fall in spirit and physically let them be destroyed over the water in the calabash. After purification bathe with the water in the bucket and retain some for drinking, after that use incense of victory. Throw the water in the calabash outside or where you know that your enemies will step.[32]

For power over the evil spirit one should read Psalms 104, three times, 71 once, 53-55 once, 130 seven times and 137 three times for three months. These Psalms must be read into water for bath for three months. The water should be used for bathing every week. It could also be simply read everyday as prayer. If one has the opportunity of using candles, for further effectiveness, one should use two black candles, a yellow, orange, pink, and three white candles for both prayer and reading into water. It will destroy all evil spirit.[33] Protection against familiar spirits requires the reading of the Bible into a big pot full of water, pour into that water a perfume called *bintu (Perfume)* and then read Psalms, 3, 11, 23, 24, and 51, Leviticus 26:6-7, Proverb 3:17-24, seven times, with candles near the new pot for three days. On the third day, exactly at 12 noon, the pot should be taken to the bush where deep hole will be dug and a person with the familiar spirit should enter that hole naked. Bathe such a person in that hole and when he or she gets out of the hole, he or she should go home without looking back till he reaches his or her house. Break the pot in that hole and cover the pot. The same day a cake should be baked and the cake and some money should be given to the needy as alms. For seven days the one with the familiar spirit must not go to town and must not come out of his or her house after 7 P.M. for seven days when offering the prayers.[34]

Read Psalms 9, 27, and 68 for protection for pregnant women who have the history of miscarriage. The pregnant woman will fast till 9 A.M. of the second day. For the first day, she should get stream water and put three-palm front inside it. She should read Ps. 9, 27 and 101:1-end on the second day and Psalm 9, 68, and 101 on the third day. She should put some of the water in a cup. She would bath with the rest of the water. After the third day of bathing she should have a bucket of water, call seven or three prophets or even all the congregation, light four candles each of the four corners of the room or church for the prayers. There should be the burning of incense, singing seven songs of victory. Immediately they finish one song, they shall pray for victory, healing, redemption, and for easy and peaceful child bearing. After seven songs and seven prayers for her, read Psalms.30, 40, and 70 to bless water for her to drink and to bathe at 9 P.M.[35]

Bolarinwa also prescribed Psalm 126 as a protection for a pregnant woman. According to him,

> When a woman with past experience of infant mortality becomes pregnant she should read this Psalm into the water for her bath, wash with it and drink a little from it daily throughout the period of gestation. Immediately after delivery, the same process should continue. The Psalm should be read into water to wash the baby until it is fully grown. The possibility of early death of the child becomes remote.[36]

Isaiah 60:20, Psalms 30, and 88 are prescribed for protection against sudden death with the following special instruction below:

If thou dream that you clear your hair, see a dead person as a living person, death is before you, provide a white plate, put palm oil in it. Read Psalm. 88 three times on it and say, 'nobody weeps for death in the house of God, we never hear close feet of mourners in the house of Almighty. The name we call is Jesus Christ the Son of God, the savior of the world that he saves the earth from spoiling.' Read Psalm 30 seven times to oil, and say these words: 'The voice of singing never dies in the house of God. The lamp of Spirit never consume in the house of Almighty. The name we are calling is creator, who created the world. The king that sees man, world, and sun.' Read again Isaiah 60:20 nine times into the oil and say 'Days never finish in the house of God, the sun never set in the house of Almighty, the name we call immortality the prince of crown of heaven.' Pray seriously for victory, put it in some container, lick it and rub it over your body, no sudden death at all.[37]

Psalm 4, 8, and 28 are recommended for protection for students and against forgetfulness. Take some well or spring water. Put an unbroken egg and sugar cane inside the water. Read Psalms 4, 8, and 28 with the holy names *ELIALARO FAJA* sixteen times into a spring or well water. Pray for protection over the water and put the egg into the fire to burn off completely and bathe with the water. If all students fail and if all students die, you will be successful and not die.[38] Psalms 4, 10, 17, and 12 are prescribed for protection against poverty. Adeboyejo gives his instructions:

> If you are in long term poverty, get a bucket of water, get ripe palm fruits, snail and dry pepper, if male, get nine, if female, seven, put all in the water, read Psalm .4, Genesis 1,read all verses, Psalms. 17, 12, 74 and 10. Read them thrice each pray for victory over poverty. Pray this prayer: "God the father of host, God of the living not of the dead, God who changes poverty to happiness, God who changed the poverty of the Israelites when the people of Moab cursed them, that God who changed curses to blessing, please change my poverty to prosperity." (Take away the materials and use the water to bathe always), until change occurs.[39]

Psalms 9, 27, 51, 91, 109, Genesis 11:1-9, and Matthew 15: 29-38 are prescribed for protection against extravagance. Prophet Samuel Adewole prescribes the above passages with coconut. A hole should be made on it, pour three to seven limewater, a spoonful of ocean water, and a perfume. "Burn heavy incense and sprinkle perfume to enable the powerful angels descend." Light a candle light on the hole of the coconut which should be put on a rock. While holding three other candles in one's hand sing three songs of forgiveness and victory and seven songs of thanks and praise.[40]Recite the holy names *Jah-Jehovah, Jah-Emmanuel, Jah-Michael* seven times.[41]

Endnotes

[1]P.A Dopamu, " The Reality of Isaasi, Apeta, Ironsi and Efun as forces of Evil among the Yoruba," *Journal Arabic and Religious Studies* 4 Dec. 1987):50-61; Dopamu, "Epe: The Magic of Curse among the Yoruba," *Religions* 8 (Dec.1983),

Endnotes

1-11. Solomon Ademiluka,, "The Use of Psalms in African Context", M.AThesis, University of Ilorin, Ilorin, Nigeria, Dec. 1990,57.

[2]P.A Dopamu, *Esu: The Invisible Foe of Man* (Ijebu-Ode: Shebiotimo Publications, 1986), p. 57.

[3]Mr Tola Agoro, Delta State University, Abraka. Interviewed on 12/9/96

[4]Ademiluka, "The use of Psalms in African Context,"

[5]Ademiluka, "The Use of Psalms in African Context," 71-72

[6]Mr. Tola Agoro, Abraka, Interviewed on 12/9/96

[7]Dopamu, *Esu: The Invisible Foe of Man*, p.57.

[8]There are other important reasons for the emergence of African Indigenous Churches: national feelings, struggles for authority and leadership disagrement over finance, breaches of church discipine, polygamy, lack of adequate attention paid to dreams, prophecy, and healing ministry of both body and soul.

[9]*St. Michael Prayer Book*, 1

[10]Ibid., 12.

[11]Ibid., 16.

[12]Olatunji Joel, Israel O. Abe, and Samuel Jolugba, *Itan Igbesi Aye Ajihinrere Oni Luke Jolugba Ati aofin Ijo Pelu Awon Eto Isin Kerubu & Serafu* (Isanlu: Kerubu ati Seraful, no date), 39.

[13]J.O Ogunfuye, *The Secrets of the Uses of Psalms*, Third Edition (Ibadan: no name of the Publisher, no date), 17.

Endnotes

[14]J.O Ogunfuye, *The Secrets of the Uses of Psalms*, Third Edition (Ibadan: Ogunfuye Publication, no date), 78.

[15]No publisher, no date but only the place where the booklets are obtainable: J.C. Brothers Bookshop, 26 New Market Road, Onitsha, Nigeria.

[16]*Saint Michael Prayer Book* (Lagos, Nigeria: Neye Ade and Sons, 1988.

[17]Ogunfuye, 40; *The Uses of* Psalms, 24,29.

[18]*St. Michael Prayer Book*, 31.

[19]*The Uses of Psalm*, 44,13.

[20]Ogunfuye, 21.

[21]Ibid., 70,96.

[22]Ibid., 79, 96; *The Uses of Psalms*, 45.

[23] T.N. Adeboyejo, *Saint Michael Prayer Book*, 18;Samuel Akin Adewoye, *Awake Celetians! Satan is Nearer*, 45.

[24]Samuel Akin Adewoye, *Awake Celetians!*, 46.

[25]*The Secret of the Uses of Psalms*, 7, 35, 51-52.

[26]Ibid., 7.

[27]Ibid., 85.

[28]Ibid., 86.

Endnotes

[29]Ibid., 98.

[30]Ibid.

[31]T.N Adeboyejo, St. Michael Prayer Book, 28.

[32] Ibid.

[33]Ibid., 29.

[34]Ibid., 33.

[35]Ibd., 34.

[36]J.A. Bolarinwa, *Potency and Efficacy of Psalms* (Ibadan: Oluseyi Press, no date), 67.

[3737]T.N. Adeboyejo, *St. Michael Prayer Book*, 32.

[38]Ibid.,17.

[39]ibid., 41.

[40]*Awake Celetians! Satan is Nearer*, 42.

[41]Ibid.

84

CHAPTER VI

Reading and Interpreting the Bible For Success in Life

Success in African Indigenous System

Although the purpose of this section is to discuss various means of enhancing success in African tradition, it is important to understand the meaning of success in African tradition.

The Meaning of Success in African Indigenous Tradition

In African tradition success goes beyond mere riches or education. Success pertains to the totality of life endeavor. It concerns getting a job, obtaining promotions in job positions. If one is jobless, there is no success. If one secures a job but has no appreciable promotion on the job, there is no success. Success includes accumulation of money and riches. It includes multiplication of wives and children. Traveling on water, land, and air without accident and the achievement of the purpose of traveling is success.

Success in love relationship is important one and is cherished. Divorce is lack of success in marriage and in life. Disharmony in marriage life is lack of success. Inability to find a wife or husband is lack success. If one does not find someone to love him or her is attributed to lack of success. Victory over bad habit is regarded as success. Winning court cases is success in life. Lack of success involves finding one in jail. Passing examinations is an important aspect of success. Dropping out of primary, college, or university is lack of success. Completion of training by apprentices is success.

Finding favor in the sight of God and people is success. In African indigenous tradition, that God is the author of all kind of success is not disputed. It is believed that without God no one can really achieve success. What I am trying to say is that success affects the totality of life and is taken very seriously. All means are used to enhance success. Apart from hard work, medicine such as prayer, rituals, potent words, and faith in God are employed. All these, according to African understanding, are medicine.

Means of Enhancing Success in African Indigenous Tradition

The same methods that were used for protection are also applied in order to be successful. One important way by which African indigenous people attempt to enhance success is the use of medicine called *awure* in Yoruba language of Nigeria. It literally means something that activates success or what uncovers success. This type of medicine that brings good luck may be in the form of potent words, indigenous soap, or a mixture of herbs and other ingredients to make a concoction. Whenever an important venture is being embarked upon, there is a strong awareness that enemies (man or spirits), seen, and unseen, are struggling to forestall the venture. This thought is indisputable in a typical African traditional society. Hence, when an important venture like business, building houses, taking a new wife, looking for a new job or attending an interview, is to be embarked upon, a medicine-man is often consulted to narrow down the chances of failure and increase success.

Success in Examination

African indigenous medicine for activating or improving memory abounds. Such medicine among the Yoruba people of Nigeria is called *isoye*. *Isoye* in Yoruba literally means "quickening the memory or intelligence."[1] Below is an example of such medicine prescribed by a traditional healer to one of my former student for success in examination:

> A combination of honey, *eeran* leaves, *awerepepe* leaves and one alligator pepper. All should be burnt together and mixed with honey. The client licks from the concoction and spit it into his left palm. There is a firm assurance that the client will be successful in any examination.

Success in Securing Employment

For success in securing employment, one should use the following:

> Collect pepper fruit leaves, a palm kernel, a half penny salt, seven candles and a basin. The palm kernel should be broken into two-equal half. Chew the one on the right side. Wash the leaves in the basin and spray the basin with the chewed kernel. As the basin is sprayed with the kernel, repeat this word, *Didun ni iyo ndunbe* seven times (salt sweetens soup 7 times). One should bathe with the water in the basin while repeating the above potent words. There is assurance that one would secure a job.

Success for Good Sale or Riches

There are potent words that can be used to increase one's chances of good sales or riches. Pastor Tola Agoro gave me the example of this indigenous means of using powerful words:

Agb e ti o ni oro, Ki i rahun aro	Agbe bird who owns dye does not complaint the lack of dye
Aluko ti o ni osun, ki rahun osun	Aluko bird that owns *osun* does not complaint the lack of *osun*
Lekeleke ki i rahun efun	Lekeleke bird does not complaint
Agbe ni gbe agbe de igbo aro	The destiny of agbe leads the lack
Alakanle ni ti osumare	Osumare is always in possession of chalk
Arira ma je ki nrahun owo	Arira do not let me complaint of lack of money

Arira ma je ki nrahun omo	Arira do not let me complaint of lack of children
Arira ma je ki nrahun ola	Arira do not let me complain of lack of riches
Arira ma je ki nrahun aso	Arira do not let me complain of lack of clothes

Other potent words for good luck among the Yoruba people of Nigeria are as follows:

Ori *Aluko ni gbe aluko de iju osun*	The destiny of *aluko* leads aluko to brown forest
Ori lekeleke ni ngbe lekeleke de okun efun	The destiny of *lekeleke* leads *lekeleke* to the sea of white feathers
Ori mi gbe mi de ibi rere	My destiny lead me to fortune

Another potent words used like the above to enhance success is as follows:

Ori mi o se rere fun mi	My destiny gives me fortune
Eleda mi se rere fun mi	My creator gives me fortune
Ori oka ni nsaanu oka	Oka's destiny has mercy on *oka*
Ori ere ni nsaanu ere	The destiny of a python has mercy on python
Afomo ope ni saanu ope	Parasite of a palm tree has mercy on palm tree
Ori mi o se rere fun mi	My destiny gives me fortune

These words are to be chanted early in the morning before going out for business. The belief that one would have great fortune is strong and it is never doubted.

There is also another category of medicine in Africa that is prepared for no specific ailment but for the purpose of enhancing progress in life or the realization of life aspiration. In Yoruba language they are called *awure*. In Urhobo language they are called *umwu/uhavwu*[2]

Success in Court Cases

Uproot a lawn grass with the left foot raised up. Tie a knot with the hairs on the forehead of a native cow and repeat seven times while tying this knot.[3] Put this knot in a pocket and recite the saying in your mind while going to court or going to face a panel that "It is the forehead of the native cow one only looks. No one can do anything to it." The holder of this knot must not greet anybody on his way to court until he has faced the court or panel.[4] For one to be successful in a court case or for one's case to be forgotten there is another indigenous prescription:

Collect the head of a bush fowl, a padlock, seven alligator pepper fruit, and black and white thread. One should tie the head of the bush fowl with the black and white thread to the padlock. Spray the alligator pepper on the tied padlock and the bush fowl while repeating these words:

Erin joko tan modu modu (Elephant ate all the crops in the farm).
Efon joko tan modemode (A buffalo ate all the farm crops completely). *Ko si ohun ti a fi da* (No court case for that).

One should throw this padlock and the bush fowl into the sea or bury it in the ground. The accused or the defendant would be freed or the case will be dismissed.

Success in loving a woman or man

Potent words for love are in abundant in African tradition. If one finds it difficult to get the attention of a woman, the powerful words with the name of the man or woman would help win his or her love. The charmer should go early in the morning without talking to any person. He should chew seven or nine allegator pepper, cut a pin pine tree and spit the allegator pepper on it and chant the following words and return to bed immediately.[5]

Were were ni s'aya ojo,
Were were ni s'aya osupa
Foju sona ni S'aya agbonniregun
Iwo omo (name the woman or man)
Bi o ba foju sona, ti o ko ba ri mi
Gbingbin ni epin pin ma nsun gbingbin

Shortly, the man or woman would come seeking after the charmer.

Reading and Interpreting the Bible for Success

Some Psalms were identified by the Christian converts and used with some indigenous materials. The Psalms that are identified as success Psalms are Psalms believed by the African Indigenous Churches to have the power to bring success if used with faith, rituals, such as prayer, fasting, and rehearsal of some specific symbols, and a combination of other animate or inanimate materials. Christians in Africa who were not comfortable with using pure indigenous ways of obtaining success mostly because of its condemnation by the western orthodox Christians and missionaries, had no choice but to find the alternative method of achieving success. They turned to the Christian Bible, and found similar words, especially in Psalms. This led to the aggressive search of the Bible for potent words. This search was accompanied by faith that the word of God must be powerful.

Success in Examination

For success in studies and/or examinations, Psalms 4, 8:1-9; 9; 23; 24; 27; 46; 51; 119:9-16,134 are identified. For students who want to improve their memory and be sure of success in all their examinations Psalms 4 should be used with this instruction.

The student should cut four candles into three each. He or she should light them round and be in the middle of the candles. Put some salt under each candle and then read Psalm 4 eight times calling the holy name *Alatula Ja Ajaralhliah* seventy two times.[6] In order to sharpen one's memory, Psalms 9, 24,27, and 46 are recommended by the Prophet Sam Akin Adewole with specific instructions to be followed.[7] Seven coconut juice should be used to boil three native eggs. The water should be kept safe in a bowl and the eggs should be in another white dish with honey close to it. Light seven candles round the students, preferably in the mercy land or in the prayer room. Burn heavy incense and sprinkle original perfume. Sing three songs for the forgiveness of sin, three for mercy, and the last for thanks. Pronounce the holy names of God, *Jah-Jehovah* seven times, and Jesus Christ. Holy Mother Mary (7 times), *Jehova Shico Horamy, Jehovah Elion, Jehovah Jireh, El-brakah-bred-El* (7 times). Read also Psalms 51, 27, 24, 46, 9; Isaiah 60; II Chronicle 9:13-28.

He also recommends Psalm 8:9 for success in examinations with instructions. The name of the school where the examination would be taken should be written on a parchment paper. At the bottom of that paper, write Psalms 8:1-9 with the holy names of God: [8]

> *Jah- Jubrillah*
> *Elli- Appejubba*
> *Elli- Majjubbah*
> *Elli- Jah-Bubbih*
> *Elli- Ilah* (mention the name of the person) and where he/she is going to take examination.

Recite another holy name, *Jehovah-Ellisaittah* three times with Amen Selah. Then burn the paper to ashes, divide it into two. Put one into water for drinking before going into the examination. Put the second one into olive oil or *bintu* for anointing before the examination. Success is guaranteed.

For general rememberance, it is important to read Psalm 6 with specific instruction. Fast for a whole day. In the middle of the night before the fast, pray at 6 am, 12 noon, and 6 pm. Read Psalm 6 three times over an egg. Break the egg and use the white water inside the egg to rub ones armpit and in order to remember what has been learnt.

According to Prophet Adewale, Psalm 119:9-16, Deuteronomy 33:1-3, Joshua 1:1-8 are for improved memory. Cook one local egg. After removing its shell, put it in a cup or glass of water and read the above passages over the water and the egg. Eat the egg, and drink the water. Or one may read the Word of God over honey or olive oil for drinking or licking.[9] According to him, Psalm 119:9-16, Deuteronomy 33:4, and Joshua 1:1-8 should be read on Thursday during fasting for memory, wisdom, and knowledge. At exactly 6 pm on Thursday, put the egg in a cup of water and read these passages on it with the holy names, *Kosniel, Skrunniel, Mupiel.* Pray for wisdom and knowledge and memory, then eat the egg and drink the water in the cup. At the end of the fast on Thursday read Psalm 119:9-12 three times.[10] Adewole further recommends Psalm 51, I King 3:1-14 and Psalm 23 for students who want to improve their memory. According to him, early in the morning before a student talks to any one the student should draw water and pour 3 coconut water with 7 cubes of sugar, honey and salt. The student should stand naked and undisturbed and read Psalm 51, I King 3:1-14, Psalm 23 to water. Call the names *Jehovah Emmanuel* (7 times), Holy Mother Mary (7 times), and *Jehovah Ellion* (7 times). The water should be kept in the bottle for drinking for seven days.[11]

Adeboyejo further prescribes I Kings 5:15, Daniel 1:3-20, Isaiah 42:1-9 for humility, wisdom and memory with some special prayer. The above Bible passages should be read as prayer or read into water for bathing and drinking with the following special prayer.

> God of all blessings and Creator of universe and human being whom you gave wisdom to be king of all creeping nature. Thou command that man should lord in the world in Holy Character, judgment of what is right. Lord God Almighty please give me understanding. Thy advice from above and not remove me in the presence of Thy children. I am Thy

servant and deliver thy message. I am a human being, keep me in Thy law, give me wisdom, spirit of knowledge from heaven. I know that nothing is hidden from Thee and they are clear to Thee. Let Thy wisdom and power enlighten me in my work, protect me in all my troubles, let me seek Thee this hour. Lord I will seek Thee in Thy Temple always till the end of my life. My heart is happy on Thee Lord of Glory, as a ripe banana Thou art my Father and God, my shepherd, who help me always. Thou made and keep me. Teach me Lord all your commandments, open my eyes to see Thy wondrous works.

Remember Thy promises Lord, teach me what I will talk, show me Thy way and teach me Thy righteousness, I am Thy servant teach me to like what Thou like, give me Thy help, let happiness and new spirit abide in me. Thou love the world and put Thy Holy Spirit in everything, teach me to do what will make Thee happy. Let Thy Holy Spirit guide me in Thy way. I know without Thee man is void in his way, as I see light let anything I handle result in success. Don't allow evil spirit reign over me. Teach me completely. I have faith that you shall direct me to the true way. Thou art the Lord God who helped me. From Thee I am expecting all good things. Give me thy blessing Lord. Thou art my light and Thou will turn my darkness to light. Be with me in thy way and at thy judgment give me thy Grace and Faith to my understanding, hear my prayer Lord and save me. Show me Thy way Lord so that I may walk in Thy Salvation for ever by Jesus Christ Lord our Saviour. Amen

Evangelist Luke Jolugba recommends Psalm 17 and 78 for wisdom and understanding and sharpening the memory.[12]

Securing the Love of a Woman or Man

Psalm 133 is a Psalm classified as the one that will aid one to secure love of a woman or a man. For example, if any man is looking for a girl friend or a lovely wife and has a history of failure in such endeavor; if a wife is loosing the love of her husband; if a husband is looking for the love of his wife who is probably at the verge of divorcing him, he should read this Psalm with the following important instruction:

Draw some water with your mouth into a bottle. Put some water that will fill the bottle into a bowl. Wash your face and armpit seven times in the water in the bowl. Add that water in the bow to the one in the bottle to fill it up. Then call the name of the woman/man and the name Eve/Adam 21 times. Read Psalms 133, Ruth 1.16-17 and Solomon and

> John 1.1-4 into the water at midnight and if the person is known give the
> water to her/him to drink.[13] Chief Oguntuye recommends this Psalm 133
> for husband and wife, family, society church to avoid disharmony.[14]

Adeboyejo[15] recommends Psalms 23 and 24 for any man looking for a lovable wife. To this, one should fast for a day and pray three times on that day at 6. am, 12 noon, and 6 pm. Psalms 23 and 24 should be read three times with the following holy names three times: "*HOLY MICHAEL HOLY GABRIEL. HOLY RAPHAEL HOLY URIEL ROLLER.*" Mention also *HOLY HADOOJA* three times and read Psalms 46 three times. Pray for the wife you want to marry three times on that day. One should remain at home throughout the fasting and praying. It is guaranteed that within three months lovable wife from God would come. Adeboyejo[16] also prescribes Song of Songs 3 and 8:6-8, Hosea 3:1-4 for love of a woman. Some instruction must be followed. There should be a long white thread enough to tie a woman and a man together three or four times, a bottle of white water and ocean water cover the mouth of the bottle. Read Song of Songs 3: and 8:6-8, Hosea 3:1-4 seven times on it with the names *ELI-RABAI* and *ELI- ALAROH* seven times to the water. Before reading the Bible one should offer a prayer for God to tie a man and woman together with the tread of love. Then tie the bottle of water and hang for 33 days so that it does not touch the ground. The woman should drink it until it remains small.

Prescription for marrying a good wife is as follows:[17]

> One bottle of Olive Oil, light three candles near it. Read Ps. 51 three
> times. Ps. 130 once and Ps. 24 pray for forgiveness of sin, use this Holy
> Name *JOFE* to read Ps. 8, 21 times around 9 pm at night use *CHANNAJA*
> to read Ps. 5 seven times around 5 A.M in the morning and read Ps 45
> seven times over the oil, as you are reading these Ps mention the name of
> the girl you want to marry, you will do this for three days, use the olive
> oil to rub your body.

Psalm 51 and Song of Solomon 3 could also be read three times over olive oil or water for the beloved for drinking while one is in the middle of a circle drawn with a chalk and call the holy name *DODIM*.[18]

One of the common problems in African tradition is for a wife to run away from their husbands' home. Prophet Adegboyejo[19] has special Bible reading for run away wife to return to the husband is Ezekiel 16:8-14, 36:23-28, Isaiah 35 and 54:4-17, Gen. 28:15, Ps. 26, 45, 97,98, 126, 20 and 24 and 140 with some specific instruction. One should dig a hole in front of the woman's room call the names of *Jehovah Bahaba Tahuboh* seven times in to that small hole. If the woman ran away because the husband is poor, let the man read Ezek. 16:8-14, Isaiah 54:4-17, Isaiah 35, Gen. 28:15, Psalm 20, 24, 126. Special prayer should be offered for seven days that she should come back. But if the woman ran away as result of the man's carelessness, the husband should add Ezek. 36:23-28 to the above reading and pray that God would return her home immediately. One should use seven candles for this prayer. It is certain that the woman would return within seven days. Immediately the woman returns home, bury the remaining candles in the hole and pray with the wife for genuine love and read Psalm 45, 26, 97, 98, 140.

While Prophet Adeboyejo recommends Psalm 111 for those who are unsuccessful in finding wives.[20] Ogunfuye recommends 45 and 46 for harmony between husband and wife.[21] According to him, if a man wishes peace and harmony between himself and his wife, Psalm 45 should be read into olive oil and then allow his wife to anoint her body with the concentrated oil.[22] If there is a misunderstanding between husband and wife caused by the husband Psalm 46 should be read over olive oil, the wife to anoint herself with the olive oil for forgiveness. He also prescribes Psalm 97 and 98 for harmony among church members.[23]

Prophet Sam Adewole[24] also recommends Psalms 51, 133 and Isaiah 60 for securing the love of a woman or a man. Use the following instruction. Sew blue cloth on four corners. Buy coconut. Write his or her name three around the coconut with a biro three times. Make three signs of the cross around the name. Burn incense and sprinkle original perfume. Call these holy names: *Jehovah, Jehovah Emmanuel, and Jehovah Nissi* twenty-one times. Read Psalm 51, 133, and Isaiah 60. In another booklets called the Revelation of God for 1992, he identifies Psalms 13, 51,to be read 13 times, and 133 to be read 21 times for love of a woman or a man. According to the prophet, one should use early morning water or direct rain that falls especially on Wednesday or Sunday. After calling the names Holy Mary (21 times), *Jehovah Jire* (21 times) on the water, drink it.[25]

Success in Court Cases

As mentioned above, winning court cases is part of success. Reading passages of the Bible and a combination of other materials can be used to win cases.

Whenever it is three days to go to court for a specific case, fast for three days. After that stand in the midst of the congregation with a sincere confession of sins silently. Let all the congregation prays for you. Before the case starts, take one coconut, three candles and a big stone. Light the candles before starting the ritual. Break the coconut on a big stone. Read Psalms 13, 51, 77, 83, 110 seven times. Read also Psalms 35 and 148 three times. Call the names Holy Michael to the East, Holy Gabriel to the West, Holy Raphael to the North, and Holy *Uriel Roller* to the South. With the Holy Name *Jehovah-Aturakaja* seven times. Say the case of (your name) and (the other person's name) becomes...*WOMWOMWOB* seven times. Let me win. While holding the coconut, say that the day that any coconut knocks the stone it will break into pieces. Then knock the coconut very hard on that stone by force and say IN THE NAME OF JESUS CHRIST while knocking the coconut on the stone.[26] However, for winning court cases, Evangelist Jolugba recommends Psalm 44 and 72.[27] Prophet Adewole in his own recommendation identifies Psalms 7, 10, 17, 18, 44, and 30 for success in court cases. If one wants justice to be done, the above Psalms should be read on the rock with a coconut while standing naked and calling on the names *Ell-Tubi*

(21 times), *Akabikada* (21 times), and *Ajagaturah* (21 times).[28]

Success in Business and at Work

Psalms 4, 108, and 114 are special Psalms for success in any venture one embarks on such as laying the foundation of a house, promotion in government work, embarking on a business trip. These Psalms have to be read with prescribed instruction and prayers to accompany them. Chief Ogunfuye[29] recommends Psalm 4, 114 are specifically for success in any business or in any undertaking. This Psalm has to be read with the holy name *Jehovah Sella Jiheje* including the prayers. He recommends that Psalm 4 or 114 and their prescribed prayers be written in pure parchment of paper with the holy name *Jiheje* and carried around in a pocket or bag. The prayer he recommends for this Psalm is:

> Almighty God and holy *Jiheje*, I commend unto Thee my work and all my desires. I beseech Thee in Thy great holy name to prosper my work and give me victory over all my adversaries. Crown all my efforts with success and lead me in the paths of righteousness always. Hear my prayer this morning for the sake of Thy adorable holy name Jehovah Sella *Jiheje*. Amen.[30]

Concerning the use of Psalm 114 for success in business, Ogunfuye asks the question: "Do you want success in your business ventures? Do you also want the business to grow from strength to strength?" He answers the question: "Then you have to be reading this Psalm early in the morning from time to time with the holy names *Aha* and *Adonai* in mind when the Psalm is being read. Furthermore, the prayer below should also be read in addition to the reading of the Psalm."

> My Father and my King, I humbly beseech Thee to give me Thy grace and bless me in my work. Let me receive the help and good will of all people so that my work may continue to grow bigger and stronger. Direct unto me good and reliable customers and give me Thy heavenly wisdom to direct my business according to Thy Holy will. Give me

> sound health and enough energy to run my daily race with success. Hear
> my prayer and let my supplication come before Thy throne for the sake
> of Thy holy name. Amen.[31]

For promotion at work, he recommends Psalm 75 and 132 with their specific prayers. It could be written in a pure parchment of paper to be carried around, especially while going to work. Psalm 132 will also enable ones glory to shine always and attain high post when read in the morning, afternoon, and evening for seven days.[32]

General Success and Blessing

There are Psalms that are regarded as useful for general success and progress of all kinds. Example of such Psalms is Psalms 1 and 67. Psalm 1 is to be read very often with the holy name *Eel Chad, Jehovah Shalom*. It is to be read in conjunction with some specific prayers and trust in the all-saving grace of the Almighty God. Such a person will always be successful in all his ways and whatever he sets his or her hands on will be fruitful. Below is the specific prayer to accompany the reading of Psalm 1:

> Almighty God, Fountain of all goodness,
> I beseech Thee in the name of *Eel, Chad,*
> *Jehovah, Shallom* to hear my prayers
> and lighten my ways. Let all that I ask
> for in Thy name be successful.
> Help me in all ways possible
> and let my prayers be acceptable in
> Thy sight for the sake of the great
> holy name *Eel, Chad*. Amen.[33]

For people in a high post who want promotion and honor, Psalm 92, 94, 10, 20, 23, 92, 94, and 100 should be read three times to water in a brand new pot with seven palm front. One should call the name *Jehovah Elohim* seven times and pray over the water according to one's desire. Use this water for bathing. According to Prophet Adeboyejo, one is bound to succeed. For special success and blessing at work, read Psalm 41 once on Monday early in the morning with he holy name *Eli-Elihaha Hah* eight times and said, "Lead me Oh Lord."[34] Jolugba recommends the reading of Psalm132 for those who are in business.

For general success and blessing, one should read Psalms 20 with the holy name *Ellirabbinah,* Psalms 121 with the holy name *Ellimmirrattaji,* and Psalms 131 with the holy name *Ellijjarrabbonah.* All of these should be read three times with special prayer to the Lord: "thou that blessing flow from, I raise my eyes up to Thee, have mercy upon me to receive thy merciful sight and mercy in all my life by the Grace of Thy Son Jesus Christ our Lord, Amen."[35]

Adeboyejo[36] also recommends Psalms 72 and 21. Psalm 72 should be written in parchment paper with the holy name: *Akemo Kehujjah Zerro Zerroyye* twice. The holy names should be written under the Psalm 72. One should burn the parchment and add the ashes to an olive oil while burning a candle and bless the olive oil with the reading of Psalm 21. For special wonders to happen in term of blessing and success in life use the oil to anoint the body. One can also draw the sign of the cross on a parchment paper with Psalms 119:117-24, John 17:24-26 written on the paper. The holy name *Akemoke-Hajjah, Zerro-Zeroyye* should also be written on the parchment. Burn the parchment paper and put it into olive oil for anointment.

Offer the following special prayer for seven days: "All the world want glory of sun, all the world want the glory of moon, every one to love and favor me today, in the name of Jesus Christ our Lord, Amen." Success and blessing are certain.

Psalm 14 is also good for blessing and success. After giving two ten *kobo* (Nigerian currency) as alm to beggars early in the morning, have a complete fast till 12 noon. Drink *gari* (most common food made from cassava) and banana for breakfast and read Psalms 14 thirteen times with the calling of the holy name *Alila Hola* times. Before reading the said Psalm one should have prayed for what type of blessings one wants.[37] For lack of savings or extravangace, Prophet Adewole[38] recommends Psalms 9, 27, 51, 91, 109, Genesis 11:1-9, and Matthew 15:29-38 to be read three times while kneeling down and praying directly to God for ability to save money. This should be read after some rituals and the call of the holy names *Jah-Jehovah, Jah-Emmanuel, Jah-Michael* seven times to the four corners of the world with the following instruction; Make a big hole in a coconut and add three or seven limewater, spoon full of ocean water and perfume. One should burn heavy incense and sprinkle perfume to enable powerful angels descends. Put the coconut flat on the rock with a candlelight placed exactly in the hole of the coconut. With three other candles in one hand sing three songs of forgiveness, victory and one song of thanksgiving to God.

One can make special soap for success with the reading of the Bible. According to Adeboyejo, in order to do this, one should buy sunlight soap, get rain water, ocean water, stream water, lake or pond water or from coconut juice and water from a banana tree which has been cut down. Squeeze it, mix them well with sunlight soap or pound them in a mortar. One should also buy two yards of white cloth and spread it on the floor or mat and sit on it with the mixed soap, and the different kind of water. Pray on your knees, and use the holy names *JEHOVH-JAFARAMI-ISAILABI HEJA KASABITAH.* One should also read Psalms 118, 108, 57, 41 three times. Call another holy names *JEHOVAH BIBBKAJABI RAJAH AJABIRAH* while reading Isaiah 41:10-14 and John 1:1-14. The following special prayer should accompany this reading:

No king who gives alm like Lord God Almighty, thou are Lord of everything, Lord my time is in Thy Hand, King that forgive sins Thou that forgive David Thy servant, Thou change his affliction to goodness, the king that changes weeping to laughing, that changes sorrow to happiness, thou Lord stop the mouth of teasing and contempt for Thy servant, Lord please in Thy great honour let all my enemies be ashamed I know that my Redeemer is alive. Lord God incomprehensible, I pray Thee in the Name of Thy bosom Son Jesus Christ keep the mouth of my enemy shut and change the time of my tribulation to goodness for the Name of Thy Son called Messiah Holy One, Redeemer of Israel, King of Glory, spread blessing of money on my work, to extend that there is no place to contain them, send dew of blessing on me increase my joy, increase my glory, help me to make my life to be sweet more than honey, in the Name of Jesus Christ Emmanuel Benevolence Lord and our Saviour, Amen, Read the said Psalms with prayer for three, seven or fourteen days for it as you want it to work. Bath with the soap always.[39]

Endnotes

[1] Ademiluka, "The Use of Psalms," 88

[2] ibid., 284.

[3] ibid.

[4] ibid.

[5] Pastor Tola Agoro gave me the potent words for love. He is in works department and also serves as my assistant chaplain in Delta State University Interdenominational Chapel, Abraka, Nigeria.

[6] T.N Adegboyejo, *St. Michael Prayer Book*, 23.

[7] S.A Adewole, *Awake Celetians, Satan is Nearer* (Lagos; Celetia Church of Christ, Opopo-Igbala, Ikola Rd, 1991) 45.

[8] T.N Adeboyejo, *Saint Micheal Prayer Book* (Lagos:Neye Ade and Sons, n.d), 14

[9] aibid., 33

[10] ibid., 10

[11] Prophet Samuel Akin Adewole, *The Revelations of God for 1992 and the Years Ahead Plus some Effective special Psalms to solve various Problems* (Lagos: Celetial Church of Christ, 1991), 24

[12] Luke Jolugba, *Itan Igbesi Aye Ajihinrere Oni Luke Jolugba Ati Ofin Ijo Pelu Awon Eto Isin Kerubu and Serafu,* (Isanlu: Willy Industries Printing Press, nd), 37.

Endnotes

[13] Adegboyejo, 27.

[14] *Secrets*, 88-89

[15] Adeboyejo, *Saint Michael*, 31

[16] Ibid. 32-33

[17] Ibid., 35

[18] Ibid. 46

[19] Ibid. 11

[20] Jolugba, 42

[21] J. Ogunfuye, *Secrets of the Uses of Psalms*, 31.

[22] Ibid.

[23] Ibid., 59-60

[24] Sam Adewole, *Awake Celetians, Satan is Nearer*

[25] Sameul Adewole, *The Revelation of God for 1992*, 23

[26] Adeboyejo, 31

[27] Jolugba, 39,40.

[28] Samuel Akin Adewole, *The Revelation of God for 1992*, 22-23.

[29] J.O Ogunfuye, *The Secrets of the Uses of Psalms*, (Ibadan: Pope Rising Press, nd), 4

Endnotes

[30] Ibid

[31] Ibid., 69

[32] Ibid., 41 and 88

[33] Ibid., 1

[34] ibid 17

[35] Ibid,15

[36] Ibid.

[37] Ibid.16

[38] Sam Akin Adewole, Awake Celestians! Satan is Nearer, (Lagos: nd), 42

[3939] Adeboyejo, 40

CHAPTER VII

CRITICAL EVALUATION

At a glance, the above approaches to Psalms are prone to condemnation as paganistic, magical, and syncretistic. A critical examination of the practice will show that it came as a result of the fact that converts had to search for original Christianity to deal with the old and new African problems. The discussion above is a perfect example of contextualization at work and Africans' attempt to make their own contribution to Christianity. In doing this, Indigenous African Christian recognise the fact that God's revelation at all times has never failed to take, the culture of the people into consideration in order to make them understand his message. In the Old Testament, the culture of Ancient Near East was taken seriously and used for communication to the people of Ancient Israel.

During the Greco-Roman period, the Greco-Roman culture was used for the presentation of the gospel. African indigenous Christians have taken into consideration African religio-cultural tradition in presenting the message of God since the Bible must be made to speak to the life and thought of the people in languages and images that are understood by them. The African culture, customs, traditions, arts, metaphors and image are necessary prerequisites for interpretation for African to feel at home with the gospel. This is important because African religio-cultural tradition are closer to the biblical and ancient Near Eastern culture than the Western tradition as affirmed by David Garret: " Africanism is not only good in itself, but also a culture closer than European to the biblical way of life, and therefore more suitable for building a Christian society."[1]

A close study of this book reveals that the reading and interpreting the Bible to solve individual existential problems demonstrate the powerful influence of African traditional culture and religion. It demonstrates that the African indigenous churches' attempt to indigenize or contextualize Christianity in Africa. More than anything else, the strong belief in the power of names, including the names of God and angels and even people, the belief in the power of medicine as God allows it to work, the power of words including the written word, the Bible more than anything else. Faith in God for these things to work are outstanding as it is in African indigenous religion all over.[2]

The Use of Names

A close examination of the reading and interpretation of Bible in African Indigenous Churches above shows that the use of names is predominant. Some of these names that are recited or invoked are names of God in the Old and New Testament, such as *Yahweh, Elohim, Adonai;* names of angels such as Gabriel, Michael, Uriel, and some unknown names. Such include *Alatulah, Ja, Ajarahlial, Ehala, Selidira, Tabbih, Jaschaja, Bali, Hashina Walola, Asabata Ja,* and *womwomwoba.* During my visit to some of these indigenous churches, I learned that some of the names used are names of God that describe his activities such as *Jehovah Jireh,*[3] *Jehovah Nissi, Jehovah Shallom, Jehovah Shammah, Jehovah Tsidkenu,*[4] *Jehovah Rophe,*[5] *El Shaddai , Hehovah Mkeddesh, Jehovah Rohi,*[6] *Jehovah Shaphat,*[7] *Jehovah Zadak*[8]*, Jehovah Zabad, Jehovah Emmanuel.*[9]

In addition, names of persons are generally mentioned. Although some of these names are Hebrew names from the Old Testament, they are not properly spelled or pronounced. This is probably because the users are not literate in biblical Hebrew. However, during my interview with some of the prophets and apostles of these churches, they claimed that these names were revealed to them by God. The truth is that some of these names are unbiblical and unknown to me and many other scholars and pastors of the mainline missionary churches in Africa. Despite the fact that some of these names are not known, the invocation of names in the use of Psalms is quite in line with African culture, as well as with the Bible.[10] It confirms the belief in the African tradition that names are powerful. It confirms the belief in the power of God and His name.

Among Africans, names are not only symbolic, they represents the totality of a person. The Yoruba people of Nigeria regard names as having special power. Names are chosen with great care because such names may represent one's prayer to God, to the divinities. It may be an expression of faith in the existence of *God (Orunbe)*, God's goodness (*Chukwu dima*), God's providence (*'Yiopese*), and God's love (*Olufemi*).[11] Names may represent the parents' experience in life or during birth. Most of the time names are given with special meanings. This is also true among the Ibos of Nigeria.[12] The very important and elaborate ritual called naming ceremony, performed among the Yoruba people of Nigeria signifies how important names to them.

It is also believed that the type of names given to a person may change his or her destiny. Since names represent the totality of what a person is, it is believed that if you know the actual names and appellation of a person, you can charm a person to obey your wish. Hence, when I was growing up in my village it was often emphasized that if a stranger or someone unknown calls your name, you should not answer because one's heart may be taken.

I believe that African indigenous churches, by placing so much emphasis on names and the invocation of these names of God, angels, persons in their reading of Psalms, are making effective use of the African concept of names and power. In order to demonstrate this special power in the use of the names of God and in the use of the Bible, these evangelists and prophets recommend the use of these names in conjunction with the reading of specific Bible passages.

Different names of God in the Old Testament and New

Testament are used. Christians and disciples are asked to pray in the name of Jesus and whatever is asked in Jesus' name shall be given. Although there are some strange and mysterious names, one should be cautious in outright condemnation of the use of the names of God because invocation of God's
name is biblical. This demonstrates the closeness of African culture to the biblical culture. African Christians are comfortable using these names that are believed to have abundant powers.

The Use of Medicine

The use of protective passages with medicine is an important aspect of the prescription for protection, success and healing. This includes the use of herbs, part of living and none living things in conjunction with the reading of specific Psalms, burning of candles, prayers and recitation of the names of God for certain number of times. In fact, the book of Psalms particularly is classified into protective, therapeutic, and success Psalms according to the African ways of classification of medicine. The truth is that some of the herbs used contain some potent ingredients in themselves that heal diseases. The use of non-living things may not contain any special ingredient for healing but from my interview I gathered that the use of those non-living materials like sand, stone, and others is a demonstration of faith in God's power to make those things potent. It is also a demonstration of God's power over nature. What makes the entire materials, including the Psalms, potent for healing is the demonstration of God's power and mercy. It means, therefore, that once they are blessed, God transfers His power into anything that the prophets lay their hands on. The use of herbs and other materials therapeutically does not only have African cultural basis, it also has a biblical basis. II Kings chapter 4 shows that Elisha healed the Shunammite's son simply with words in form of prayer. He healed those who ate the poisonous herbs by casting a "meal" into the pot (II Kings 4.38-49). The flowing water from river Jordan was also prescribed for Naaman to dip himself in the water 7 times and he was healed (II King 5.14). The Prophet Isaiah prescribed a lump of figs for Hezekiah with the combination of prayers for his boil and he was healed (II Kings 20.1 - 11). In the New Testament, Jesus healed the sick with a variety of methods. He healed a leper with mere pronouncement of words, "...be thou clean," and a touch (Matt. 8.3). He healed those who were possessed with evil spirit with the mere word, "Go." A blind man was also healed with saliva, clay, water and words (Jn.9.6-7). After washing in the water of Siloam, the blind man's eyes were opened. Paul, the apostle also demonstrated the use of potent words. He healed Publius who was sick of fever and bloody flux(Acts. 28.8). Peter also healed Aeneas by the use of words and the name of Jesus.[13]

The Use of the Potent words.

I have discussed above the importance of the use of potent words for healing purposes, protection, and success. It does not make sense to call African mysterious words "incantation" as labeled by the Eurocentric observers, anthropologists and sociologists. Since the early missionaries condemned the use of the so- called "incantation" for these purposes, Africans who became Christians found an alternative. I have also mentioned above that the most logical place to search for the alternative is in the Christian Bible, which, they believe, must have potent words for everyday problems of Africans. African Christians believed that the white men were probably hiding those potent words from African Christians so that they may not be as powerful as they were. The contents of some books of Psalms resemble that of African potent words for healing, for protection and success. These were memorized and used for these purposes. In experimenting with these Psalms they were found effective. One important revelation during my interview is that there was no iota of doubt as to the potency of the words of Psalms if one knows how, when, and where to read for specific problems. In the New Testament, African Indigenous Churches in Nigeria found that Jesus Christ used the word of God successfully to overcome Satan. When he was tempted he used the word of God, 'It is written, man shall not live by bread alone, but every word that proceeded out of the mouth of God' (Matt. 4.4 KJV). At the second temptation Jesus used the word of God, 'It is written again, thou shall not tempt the Lord thy God' (Matt. 4.7). During the third temptation he said, "Get Thee hence, Satan: for it is written, Thou shall worship the Lord thy God and him only shall thou serve" (Matt. 4.8). There are many other passages where Jesus used the word of God to cast out demons. Paul the Apostle, used the words of mouth to rebuke and blindfold the enemy, a sorcerer, and a child of the devil, when he was obstructing him (Acts. 13.9-11).

Endnotes

[1] Schism and Renewal in Africa (Oxford University Press, 1968), 166.

[2] Whenever the priest prepares medicine and dispense to any person, such priest in African tradition and religion always invoke the power of Almighty God (*Olodumare* in Yoruba) saying "*L'agbara Olorun*" or "*L'agbara Olodumare*."(By the power of God)

[3] The name Jehovah Jireh is to be used for special prayer to seek God's favour by reading Psalm 123.

[4] This name means God is righteous and should be used for deliverance when afflicted by principalities and

powers. It should be combined with the reading of Psalm 88. The name should be chanted 7 times.

[5] Means Yahweh Heals (Ex. 15.26) and should be used for sick persons using clear rain water in the calabash

with new palm tree leaves that points to the sky and with 7 candles round the calabash.

[6] This name means God is my shepherd and to be chanted 7 times with the reading of Psalm 23 for protection

[7] This name should be chanted 7 times with the reading of Psalm 7 for court cases.

[8] Call this name 7 times for those who hated and oppressed you unjustly with the reading of Psalm 12.

[9] The fact is that some of these names are not invented, they are biblical names in Hebrew.

[10] In the Old Testament, the proclamation of the names of God (Yahweh) is very frequent and is associated with his presence and power. See Psalms 29; 28.1; 82; 89.6ff.; 103.20; 148. Iff.;, 46.7; 48.8;59.5;69.6; 76.1; 111.9;54.1; 20.1; Isa.6.2f.; Ikings 2219;Ex.7.4; 12.41;Num. 10.36; ISam. 17.45; II Sam. 6.2. See more list of those passages in Arthur Weiser, *77,e Psalms, I 9*

[11] Unfortunately, mostof the early missionaries to Africa did not care to understand the importance of these African names, but made us change our names at random. If they had understood these names, I believe that they would have taught us to choose the equivalent in the Old Testament, There are equivalece in the Old Testament.

[12] For further details about the significance of names, consult Roland Agoro, *Sixteen Names of God* (Ibadan:Olapade Agoro Investment Co.Ltd, 1984.

[13] I have disacussed earlier the efficacy of the use of water, fasting, and faith in African indigenous culture.

CHAPTER IX

CONCLUSION

The truth is that folklores are still alive in the African Culture and in everyday life. They only went underground as a result of misinterpretation of African culture and thought in secular oriented society. What you have read is how African Indigenous churches have made use of this aspect of African culture among their congregations to create an atmosphere and a place to feel really at home. It is the account of how African indigenous churches have been able to interpret the Bible and Christianity to meet the need of African people who feel alienated, disjointed, out of pace, and who lack of growth because of their association with the theology of Western missionary churches.[1] It is how they were able to read and interpret the Bible, African culture, and religion for the purpose of healing, protecting, and achieving success in life.

Everywhere I went, there was emphasis on power in the Word of God, the holy names of God, faith, fasting and prayer. When I asked how effective these methods, they testified that it is undoubtfully effective from many testimonies they received from their congregation. The author of *The Uses of Psalms* in the preface has this to say about how effective the method is:

> To the great God, I render my sincerest thanks for allowing the "Prayer as the remedy" to be used in honour and glory of his Holy name, for many oppressions. Satan planned against his (God's) people. Since this brochure had been published, we have received and are receiving numerous letter from all over the world testifying the importance of this book because what should have taken them to the Doctor, Auguers, and Fortune Tellers has been solved through the methods of prayer in this book. It has been proved that surely prayer is the only remedy for all things to the believers.[2]

This method of Bible interpretation is not really strange among the African American readers and interpreters. When Africans were taken to the new world, they read the Bible liberatively for healing, protection, and success. It was read and interpreted for deliverance from oppression of the slave master. Great power was attributed to the Bible as it is read among African Diaspora. The Bible is used literally, and quasi-magically among the *Shango* Baptists Church in Trinidad.[3] All over Americas, the Bible is used for power and wisdom. It is not an exaggeration to say that the Bible has played a great role among African Diaspora. That they have developed a hermeneutic, not only of suspicion, but also of liberation from all evil powers that oppressed them have been demonstrated by many African American biblical scholars such as James Cone, Cain Felder, Winbush, and others.[4]

Admittedly, care must be taken so as not to have the wrong impression that I am saying that all aspects of African cultural tradition are good. African Christians must be able to sieve what is good and compatible, and throw away whichever is not compatible. This explains the need for deeper study of African cultural tradition and all aspects of African Indigenous Churches so that the world can learn from them and assist in improving these things. This is an important task that needed to be accomplished.

I hold very strongly that African resources and approaches should be subjected to rigorous scrutiny in order to assess how they could be utilized meaningfully in contemporary society. The fact is that the African indigenous churches have presented the challenge by beginning some critical thinking in their courage to separate from the mainline missionary churches after a deep reflection and self-analysis. Churches, scholars, ordinary readers need to rise up to this challenge to assist in the reconstruction of African Christianity that is African, authentic, biblical, cultural, and acceptable.

What is urgently needed is for the West and other parts of the world to join in this reconstruction for the purpose of using African value systems for the growth of Christianity in Africa. In fact, the existence of thousands of African indigenous churches tells the story of this reconstruction. They grow so rapidly despite their meeting in shacks. Many members of the mainline churches have migrated to join the African indigenous churches because these churches meet their needs. Others from the mainline missionary churches who did not join officially, patronize them in secret and still keep their membership in the mainline churches. The testimonies of members and non-members who visit these churches either at night or daytime is a powerful evidence of the effectiveness of the use of the Bible this way. Doing theology and biblical studies for its own sake and for mere academic exercise of intellectualism, as it is done in the West, have no place in African Christianity. A combination of academic, spiritual, cultural, Christ and human-centered activities are the mission of African Christianity.

I feel that there are many ways the West and the rest of the world can authentically participate in this process of reconstruction. First, the West and other Christians can continue to render assistance in training Africans Christians and scholars by offering financial aid in form of scholarship in their seminaries and universities. When this is done, they should be encouraged to conduct researches in the area of African Christianity. Second, since most of the present African biblical scholars are unable to participate in most international academic conferences because of poverty, the West and other Christians can assist in sponsorship to attend scholarly conferences where they could receive challenges and present researches of their own. Academic cooperation between African and Western universities and seminaries can be established for the purpose of researches and exchange of ideas. Third, academic visit to many African universities and seminaries, not merely for the purpose of giving (as most of the early missionaries did), but of receiving or learning from African Christianity in a firsthand setting, should be embarked upon by Western scholars. I strongly believe that there is a lot to learn from African Christianity. Many African scholars are open to suggestions.

Finally, as a friend and colleague (Prof. Knut Holter)[5] once said that, if the west continue to do biblical studies for mere academic exercise or merely for its own sake, without serious consideration for other developing continent like Africa, it would eventually be of no relevance to anyone, but itself. This is because

Conclusion

knowledge not shared is knowledge wasted.

Research on this aspect of African Christianity is indeed in its infancy. There is an urgent need for further research in this area.

Endnotes

[1] G.C Oosthuizen, "The Task of Traditional Religion in the Church's Dilema in South Africa," 277-280

[2] Anonymous author, *The Uses of Psalms*, 3.

[3] Gosnell Yorke, "The Bible in Black Diaspora," *The Bible in Africa*, 135

[4] James Cone, *The Black Theology of Liberation*; Winbush and Felder, *Stony the Road We Trod.*

[5] Knut Holter, *Yahweh in Africa*, (New York, Peter Lang, 2000)

SELECTED BIBLIOGRAPHY

Adamo, David Tuesday. *African American Heritage,* 3rd edition completely updated, Eugene, Oregon: Wipf and Stock Publishers, 2001.

__________________ Africa and Africans in the Old Testament, San Francisco: Christian University Press, 1998, reprinted by Wipf and Stock Publishers, Oregon, 2001.

__________________ Africa and Africans in the New Testament. Book manuscript to be published by Judson Press, Valley Forge, PA, 2002.

__________________ "African Cultural Hermeneutics," in Vernacular Hermeneutics edited by R.S Sugirtharajah. Sheffield: Sheffield Academic Press, 1999.

__________________ "The Problem of Translating Hebrew Old Testament into Yoruba Language of Nigeria," *The Bible Translator,* Oct. vol 35 no 4   1984

__________________ "The Church. in Africa and African Traditional Religious Beliefs and practices", Unpublished Dissertatiorn, 1985 Rel.D.. Indiana Christian University, Indianapolis.

__________________ "The Concept of Shalom in the Old Testament and in Africa," *The Bible in African Christianity: Essays in Biblical Theology.* Nairobi: Acton Publishers, 1997

__________________ "Suffering in the Old Testament,"*Bulletin of Biblical studies,* Vol.8 (Jan. - June, 1989), University of Athens

Selected Bibliography

__________________"Understanding Genesis Creation Account in an African Background" *Caribbean Journal of Religious Studies* (CJRS), Vol. 10, No. 2, (Sept. 1989)

__________________"The Images of Cush in the Old Testament: Reflections on African Hermeneutics" in *Interpreting the Old Testament in Africa.* Editors K. Holter, Mary Getui, and Victor Zinkuratired, Peter Lang Publishing Inc, New York, 2001

__________________"The African Wife of Moses: An Examination of Numbers 12:1-9," *Africa Theological Journal (ATJ)* Vol. 18 no 3. (1989) 230-237,

__________________"Deuteronomic Conception of God According to Deuteronomy 6:4 in an African Context," *Bible Bhashyam,* (1992), 55-64

__________________"The African Wife of Moses: An Examination of Numbers 12:1-9," *Africa Theological Journal* Vol. 18 no 3. (1989) 230-237

__________________ "The Black Prophet in the Old Testament," *Journal of Arabic and Religious Studies (JARS),* Vol. 4 (Dec. 1987), 1-8 University of Ilorin

__________________"The Use of Psalms in African Indigenous Churches in Nigeria," West, Gerald, Dube, Musa. Editors. *The Bible in Africa: Transactions, Trajectories and Trends.* Boston: Brill., 2000, 336-349.

Adeboyejo, T. N. *Saint Michael Prayer Book* (Lagos: Neye Ade & Sons, 1988), 21.

Ademiluka, Olusola. "The Use of Psalms in African Context," M.A Thesis, University of Ilorin, 1991

Adewole, S.A. *The Revelation of God for 1992 and the Years Ahead*

Selected Bibliography

(Lagos: Sam Adewole, 1991), 22.

__________ *Awake Celetians, Satan is Nearer* Lagos; Celetia Church of Christ, Opopo-Igbala, Ikola Rd, 1991 45-45.

Agoro, Roland. *Sixteen Names of God* Ibadan: Olapade Agoro Investment Co.Ltd, 1984.

Awolalu, J.O.*Biblical Revelation and African Beliefs* (eds) K. Dickson and P. Ellingsworth. New York: Orbis.Books, 1969

Barret, Davd.*Schism and Renewal in Africa* (Oxford University Press, 1968), 166.

Bolarinwa, J.A. *Potency and Efficacy of Psalms*(Ibadan: Oluseyi Press, n.d), 8.

Brown, Raymond. *An Introduction to the New Testament.* New York: Doubleday, 1997.

Gordon Clinard. "Biblical Preaching on Suffering," *Southwestern Journal of Theology.* (April 1963), 33-41.

__________"Biblical Preaching on Suffering," *Southwestern Journal of Theology* (SWJTH), April 1959, 20

Cone, James. *A Black Theology of Liberation.* Philadelphia: Lippincott, 1970

Cone, J. and Wilmore, G. eds., *Black Theology: A Documentary History, 1966-1979* (Maryknoll, N.Y: Orbis Books, 1979.

Dopamu, P.A. *Esu: The Invisible Foe of Man.* Ijebu-Ode: Shebiotimo Publications, 1986, 57.

117

__________ " The Reality of Isaasi, Apeta, Ironsi and Efun as forces of Evil among the Yoruba," *Journal Arabic and Religious Studies* 4 Dec. 1987:50-61;

__________ "Epe: The Magic of Curse among the Yoruba," *Religions* 8 (Dec.1983), 1-11.

Dryness, W. *Themes in Old Testament Theology* .Downer Grove: Inter-varsity Press, 1979

Eichrodt, W. *Theology of the Old Testament.* Philadelphia: The Westmister Press, 1961. Vol. 1.

Felder, Cain Hope. *Stony the Road We Trod.* (Ed.) Minneapolis: Fortress Press, 1991)

Foerster, W.editor G. Kittel, *Theological Dictionary of the New Testament,* Vol. II Translated by Geoffrey W. Bromiley, Grand Rapids: WM B. Eerdmans Publishing Company, 1982

Holter, Knut. *Yahweh in Africa. Essays on Africa and the Old Testament.* New York: Peter Lang Publishing, Inc. 2000

George Mulrain,   "Hermeneutics within a Caribean Context," *Vernacular Hermeneutics,*
ed. R.S Sugirtharajah (Sheffeild: Sheffied Academy Press, 1999

R.L. Harris, G.L. Archer, Jr and B.K. Waltke, 'Shalom', *Theological Wordbook of the Old Testament* Chicago: Moody Bible Institute, 1981, 2401. —henceforth TWOT; Colin Brown, General Editor, 'Peace', *The New International Dictionary of the New Testament.*Grand Rapids; Zondervan Publishing House, 1982

Idowu, E.B, *Olodumare God in Yoruba Belief* London: Longmans, 1962

James Weldon Johnson. ed. *The Book of American Negro Spirituals*

Selected Bibliography

New York:Viking Press, 1925

Maultsby, P.K. "Africanism in African-American Music," in *Africanism in American Culture*, Joseph E. Holloway (ed) (Bloomington, Indiana: Indiana University Press, 1990), 185-210.

Mitchell, H. *Black Preaching: The Recovery of a Powerful Art* (Nashville: Abingdon Press, 1990)

Mbiti, J.S. *Concepts of God in Africa* London: S.P.C.K., 1970

Mume, J.O. *Traditional Medicine in Nigeria* Agbarho: Jom Tradomedical Naturopathic Hospital ,1978

Robinson, W. *Suffering Human and Divine* .New York: The Macmillan Comp. 1939), 3.

Sanders, Jim. "Suffering as Divine Discipline in the Old Testament and Post Biblical Judiasm," *Colgate Rochester Divinity School Bulletin*, (1955)42.

Ubrurhe, J. " Life and Healing Processes in Urhobo Medicine," *Humanitas* (1994) vol. 1, New Series, forth coming.

Ukpong, J.S. "Can African Old Testament Scholarship escape the historical critical approach?" *Newsletter on African Old Testament Scholarship*, Knut Holter (ed.), no 7, 1999,

Ogunfuye, J. *The Secrets of the Uses of Psalms*. Ibadan: Ogunfuye Publication, n.d.

Ukpong, Justin. " Reading the Bible with African Eyes," *Journal of Theology for Southern Africa (JTSA)*, (June 1995), 3-14.

Sugirtharajah, R.S. "Vernacular Resurrections: An Introduction," *Vernacular Hermeneutics*, (ed.). Sheffield: Sheffield Academic Press, 1999.

Weiser, A. *The Psalms, Old Testament Library*, trans. By Herbert Hartwell Philadelphia: The Westmister Press, 1962

____________*Out of Depths: the Psalms Speak for us Today* Philadelphia: The Westminster Press, 1974

Westermann, Claus. *Praise and Lament in the Psalms*, translated by K.R Crim and Richard N Soulen Atlanta: John Knox Press, 1981, 52,64.

Yorke, G.L. "Biblical Hermeneutics: an Afrocentric Perspective, "*Journal of Religion and Theology*, vol 2, no 2(1995), 145-158

Made in the USA
Monee, IL
07 July 2026

56551604R00075